Renegade
SAINT

Renegade SAINT

A Story of Hope by a Child Abuse Survivor

Phil E. QUINN

ABINGDON PRESS
NASHVILLE

RENEGADE SAINT

Library of Congress Cataloging-in-Publication Data

QUINN, P. E. (Phil E.), 1950–
Renegade saint.
Bibliography: p.
1. Quinn, P. E. (Phil E.), 1950–. 2. Adult
child abuse victims—United States—Biography.
3. Child abuse—United States. I. Title.
HV741.Q57   1986   362.7′044 [B]   86-8028

ISBN 0-687-36131-1 (alk. paper)

BOOK DESIGN BY JOHN ROBINSON

This book is printed on recycled, acid-free paper.

MANUFACTURED IN THE UNITES STATES OF AMERICA

94 95 96 97 98 99 00 01 02 03 04 — 10 9 8 7 6 5 4

This book is dedicated to my brothers,
Greg and Steve,
and to all adults everywhere
who continue to pay a price
for once having been a
child.

CONTENTS

Endless days and soul-searching nights have been spent writing this book. To choose from life's innumerable experiences those most suited for the purpose of this book is no easy task. I could not have done it alone. I turned to my dear friends Becky Rothman, Judie Holland, and Vicky Agee for guidance and support during times of greatest doubt and uncertainty. They gave me their wisdom, their suggestions and insights, making possible the selection of the essential from the unnecessary. To each of them I offer my heartfelt thanks.

To all of you who have written to me—supporting, encouraging, pushing me to tell the rest of the story—I owe this completed book. Without your interest and requests, it never would have been written.

Above all others, I owe my greatest thanks to my two younger brothers, to whom this book is dedicated. It was they, whose suffering was no less than my own, who gave me reason to continue. For each of them, like me, continues to pay a price for once having been a child.

If you read my first book, *Cry Out!: Inside the Terrifying World of an Abused Child,* you know me as Peter. You also know I was a victim of severe abuse as a child. You first met me on a cold, stormy night when I was barely five years old. That night was filled with forces I could neither control nor understand—forces that would sweep away my childhood and bring me face to face with a future so uncertain that mere survival became my preoccupation for the next twelve years. Never again would my life be the same. Never again would I know the warmth and security of a family.

Perhaps you shared my terror as I huddled with my younger brothers in a back bedroom, hearing the angry, violent words and not knowing what would happen next. Maybe you shared my grief as I watched my father leave for the last time. Were you there when the state Child Welfare Department came to take me away? Were you with me as I hid under the bed, clinging desperately to the rusty bedsprings, trying in the only way I knew how to stay with my mother? Does the taste of a chocolate milkshake fill you with the bitterness of betrayal, as it does me?

Even today, I am filled with pain when I remember trying to show my mother how much I could help her by washing the dishes and mopping the kitchen floor, in the infantile hope that she would not send me back to the farm. How well I remember the panic, the fear, the desperation of that moment! I also remember the agony in my mother's eyes as she turned away.

Do you remember Bo? What a wonderful creature he was—God's gift to a frightened, troubled little boy who needed so much what Bo had to offer! I have never forgotten Bo, our special place under the back porch, and our spot in the woods near the river. Not so long ago I revisited that farm. The memory of Bo was everywhere. How I ached to

11

hold him just one more time, to share just one more sunrise with him!

If you were able to continue reading, you remember what came next. My brothers and I were adopted and taken far away from all we had known. Then began the awful beatings, the emotional and sexual abuse. Many of you have written in an attempt to share my pain, and to express your own. You will never know how much those letters have meant to me!

As you recall, I was finally thrown out of that adoptive home. At the age of seventeen I found myself on the street, alone, with nowhere to turn. I survived in the only way I could. Ignored by the world around me, I accepted an invitation from a group of bikers to become one of them.

At that point, the first book ended. But it certainly was not the end of Peter. He is now eighteen years older, and in order to fulfill the purpose of that first book, the rest must be told. *Renegade Saint* picks up the story where *Cry Out!* left off and brings it up to date. As in *Cry Out!* most names and locations have been changed.

That first book was an attempt to describe the miserable reality of child abuse as experienced through the eyes of the innocent, helpless victim. It was my hope that by vicariously experiencing the pain and horror of such needless tragedy, more of us would be inspired to become involved in the prevention of child abuse.

The experiences I chose to describe were my own. I chose them not because they were unique or unusual, but because they were the ones I knew most intimately. Sadly enough, they are not unusual. The truth is that they are not uncommon at all. Every day, thousands of children experience similar or worse abuse at the hands of family members. Many of those children will not live to see a fifth birthday. Others will become physically or mentally disabled for life.

The purpose of that first book was to cry out for mercy and compassion on behalf of all children everywhere, especially the nameless, faceless thousands who are at this very moment experiencing untold agony at the hands of their families or guardians. It was an attempt to make the screams of our children heard above the roar of the many other social concerns of our day.

Through the combined voices of thousands of adult survivors, the cries of our children are at last being heard. Not only are they being heard in state and local governments, courts, and agencies, but more important, they are being heard in the hearts and minds of many American parents. It is there, in parents' relationship with their children, that we hope to be heard most clearly. For it is there, more than anywhere else, that child abuse can best be prevented.

If the purpose of *Cry Out!* was to inspire us to become involved in the prevention of child abuse, the purpose of *Renegade Saint* is to warn us about what may happen if we do not. It is foolish to think that children who grow up in abusive environments will develop into healthy, well-adjusted, responsible adults. Most do not.

In terms of human suffering and taxpayers' dollars, the cost of dealing with the consequences of child abuse is incredible. Our prisons are filled with maladjusted individuals who have acted out the horrors of their childhoods upon an innocent, unsuspecting society. Our mental-health system is overwhelmed by countless patients whose nightmarish memories pervade and distort their adult lives. Our social agencies deal daily with the multitudes of walking wounded who managed to survive, only to find they cannot adequately care for themselves. Tragically, the impact these maladjusted and desperate individuals can have on society is often as destructive as the effect their parents had on them.

I have been spared the fate of most victims. I have been able to break the cycle of violence and abuse in my own life, and my greatest desire is that this book will provide an element of hope for others—hope that their suffering can end; that the pain and the memories can be buried in the long-ago past; that they can at last be free of their childhoods and live healthy adult lives—but especially, hope that their children will not be abused as they were abused. As witnessed in my own life, there is hope!

The experiences you will read about here are my own. They are typical of the experiences of many survivors of severe child abuse. What is not typical, however, is that I have survived so well. There are reasons for that, as you will see.

My sincere hope is that all of us will come to appreciate the wisdom of *preventing* child abuse rather than *paying* for its consequences. Out of such wisdom will come our redemption.

PART ONE

SATAN'S SAINTS

Introduction

Shortly after the last beating his adopted parents inflicted upon him, Peter was told to leave home and never return. He was seventeen. Something about him had changed during those years of violence. He was now tall, his young, adolescent body strong and quick. But it was not his stature that frightened his parents that night. It was his attitude. He did not cower and submit helplessly, but stood tall and erect, his eyes burning a hole in the wall as blow after blow pounded the all too familiar pain into his body. Those eyes could no longer hide the seething rage and burning hatred. His parents saw that deadly intent, recognized it for what it was, and did what they had to do to protect themselves. They threw him out.

Once on the street, with no money and the knowledge that there would be no turning back, Peter sought ways to survive. After two weeks of living on scraps scavenged out of garbage cans, unable to find work, he was rescued by Satan's Saints, a group of bikers.

Although Peter accepted their help, at first he had no intention of joining their ranks. He was not even sure they would want him. Instead, he tried to join the military. He wanted a gun in his hands for only one reason—to kill people. He wanted to make other people hurt as he had hurt. By the age of seventeen, Peter had been beaten into a homicidal rage.

The armed forces, however, would not take him; he was blind in his left eye. Rejected by his family, by society, and now by the military, Peter had little choice. He joined the bikers and, after the initial doubts and uncertainty, plunged headlong into molding himself into one of them. His thoughts, feelings, and appearance all changed so he could fit in. More than anything else, he wanted to belong to someone, something, somewhere.

Like most victims of severe childhood trauma, Peter's personality had become distorted. What he had learned as a child, he continued to believe as an adolescent and as a young adult: The world around him was a hostile place to which he did not belong; other people were untrustworthy and rejecting; he himself was totally inadequate, unworthy of love and acceptance. So his life continued with but one primary purpose—to survive.

Survivors of severe child abuse tend to have a strong resentment toward authority—any authority, but particularly that which they perceive to be unjust and directed toward them. Children learn to respect authority through their relationship with their parents. If all is as it should be, children learn to trust their parents for protection and for providing their needs. If those needs are not met, however, children quickly learn that in order to survive, they must take care of themselves. Since they cannot trust their parents to take care of them, they cannot afford to respect parental authority, for to do so would threaten their survival. This attitude of self-sufficiency and distrust of authority usually will be carried into their adult lives. Trust and respect die at the hands of betrayal. And abused children are betrayed children.

Even as adults, people like Peter tend to still perceive themselves as victims. They continue to feel helpless in the face of life's demands. Unable to live up to the expectations of their parents, they have developed a life script of failure. As victims, they do not have the power either to control or to change their lives. In order to survive, then, they cannot afford to assume responsibility for their own lives. To do so would be to court failure.

Unable to win parental approval, they become convinced they cannot win social approval. They learned as children that to win approval involves living up to another's expectations. Yet to attempt to do so only invites disappointment and failure, and they cannot take the risk of more rejection. So most do not try. Believing they cannot earn approval, they tend to seek attention through disapproval.

Most survivors of severe child abuse suffer from an inner emptiness. They are lonely, desperate people who cannot form close relationships. In order to have an intimate relationship with another person, there must be trust. Yet in order to survive, they must trust no one. Many evolve into sociopaths who perceive other people as enemies, threats to their survival.

But at the same time, they are dominated by a deep sense of guilt. They blame themselves for their childhood abuse. If they had not been so bad, they believe, their parents would not have needed to beat them. They feel a need for punishment. Arrogance and defiance often shroud their sense of personal guilt—guilt for having been a child.

Raised in the midst of domestic and personal chaos, many of these people also have a desperate need for structure in their lives. They need someone to take care of them. Some are most comfortable and feel most "at home" in prison.

On top of everything else, they tend to be deeply emotional. Their emotions are not glowing embers, but raging fires. They often express themselves in violence. Perhaps this is why over 90 percent of the 1,500 individuals on death rows in this country, and over 80 percent of those who commit violent crimes were severely abused as children.

Most of these people feel they have nothing to lose. They lost it all a long time ago. So they tend to maintain a high-risk posture toward life and other people. There is no one more dangerous than someone who has nothing to lose.

Perhaps most tragic of all, adult victims of severe child abuse tend to see life as "luck." They are constantly in search of the pot of gold at the end of the rainbow. Unable to take control of their lives and successfully direct them toward goals and achievements, they rely on chance for all rewards. The result is that they tend to seek gratification wherever they may happen to find it, regardless of the consequences.

Peter was no exception. He was a survivor. It did not take him long to become totally submerged in the biker life-style. He became one of them in every respect except one—a faint, intangible flicker of hope! A hope that perhaps someday he would find someone who would love him, accept him, believe in him, and—even more important—someone he could trust and love in return. It was a dim hope that someday he could prove to himself and to the world that he was not all bad, that he could be a good and responsible person, deserving of respect. It was a hope that someday he might have, with another person, what he had had with Bo. It was a faint hope, but a hope that just would not die.

One

"Hey man! She's checkin' you out again. Look at her. She wants you, man!" whispered Buck knowingly. "She's yours for the takin', man, all yours!"

Peter shifted away from the wine- and cigarette-fouled breath so near his cheek, keeping his eyes on the young girl alone by the fire. She looked out of place—like a flower among weeds.

He watched curiously as she rejected the advances of one biker after another, each seeking a mate for the night among the females who had arrived earlier in the day. Competition was strong. There were not enough women to go around.

Some would have to be shared. Or some of the men would have to sleep alone. That could be dangerous. Wars had started over less. It was the last night of the annual holiday happening. No one wanted to be alone on the last night in camp.

Peter knew the girl would not be alone long. Her freedom to choose a partner would be surrendered if she did not exercise it soon. Remaining unattached would make her community property. Already he could sense the growing anticipation in the men hovering around him as their eager, impatient eyes watched her every move.

It was the Fourth of July weekend. Local radio stations and major rock-star promoters had sponsored the traditional holiday rock concert. Among the thousands of young people who had flocked to the three-day event, bikers from all over the state were gathered in reunion as a show of unity and force. Driving all others out by their presence, they had taken over a public campground high in the mountains, a few miles north of the nearest town and only minutes from the site of the concert. Representatives in large numbers from every major club in the area had come, each flaunting his club's colors while parading his polished, powerful, chopped Harley "hog" for all to see and admire.

Most came to party, to enjoy the weekend of music, drink, drugs, and sex. Others came to renew old friendships, to strengthen communication networks, or to expand business opportunities for their clubs. All came to profit from the weekend. The demand for drugs would be great, the supply limited, the profit high. It was an opportunity to refill depleted club coffers that few could afford to miss.

For two days Peter had watched and listened. Although he enjoyed the music, it bothered him, as it always did, that he had little interest in what seemed so important to the others. He wanted desperately to be like the others, to look and behave and think and feel like one of them. But try as he might, something was missing. It was that something that kept him apart, different, like an outsider looking in. It was that same something that drove him into the woods alone to walk for hours, thinking. Always thinking . . . endless thoughts . . . haunting thoughts. And occasionally those thoughts would spill over into poetry, which he kept well hidden in a small notebook buried deep in his hip pocket. The others would not understand.

Now the weekend was almost over. Despite the stupor and fatigue that results from two days of overindulgence, the last night of any happening was always the most exciting. Driven by a now-or-never attitude, the partying often became intense, frantic, sometimes brutal, an attempt to crowd as much into the few remaining hours as mind and body could stand.

Peter watched closely as the leader of a rival club approached the girl, only to walk arrogantly away a moment later, leaving a trail of curses in his wake. Peter could not help pitying her. She looked so young and innocent, so helpless and unprepared for what would soon happen. He had seen girls like her at other biker gatherings. Lots of them—runaways mostly. Or rebellious adolescents drawn to the event by some lurid fascination with the biker image made romantic by a Hollywood actor. Some were attracted by the freedom from parental control the biker way of life seemed to promise. Still others came seeking to become a part of something more powerful than themselves, more important than their own lives—something that would give them a reason for living, bring order to the chaos and confusion of so many whys. Then there were those like Peter, who came looking for a place to belong.

For whatever reasons, the girls always came. Usually in carloads. Many were veterans of other happenings and knew what to expect. For others, like the girl by the fire, it was their first time. Peter pitied her vulnerability. But he resented her even more. She was female. His attraction to her only reminded him how desperately he needed someone to love him. That hurt. It also frightened him. No longer did he trust women. How many times had a woman come into his childhood, only to be torn abruptly and permanently away?

Smoldering with a sudden rage, Peter stood up, causing a stir in the crowd of men lounging around him, much as a flock of geese is stirred by one taking flight. Suddenly he wanted to hurt the girl, make her suffer as he had suffered.

"You goin' to get her, man?" asked Buck eagerly as he stood up beside Peter.

"Can we have her when you're done?" asked Moose on his left as he offered Peter the marijuana butt held greedily between grimy thumb and forefinger.

"For the right price, maybe," Peter answered, not taking his burning eyes off the girl.

Peter stood a head taller than most of the men around him. His shoulder-length hair was longer, his beard shorter. He wore a rattlesnake headband, its rattles dangling down the back of his neck. Like the others, he wore the same jeans he had arrived in two days before, riding boots, and, of course, his colors, the sleeveless jean jacket with the club emblem on the back. His vest was open in front, exposing a large gold cross suspended from a chain, lying snugly against his chest. He had stolen it from a pawnbroker months before. That same day, he had pulled up behind a car with a bumper sticker that read, "Honk if you love Jesus!" Peter had honked. The driver, a young woman, had stuck her head out the window and bombarded him with a barrage of curses, accompanied by an obscene gesture. Peter wore the cross to remind him of that event and the hypocrisy it represented.

To the casual observer, Peter looked like all the others—except for his fingernails and eyes. His nails were clean, and his undilated pupils brought a clarity that could not hide the passion burning deep within—a passion the others recognized as dangerous but could not understand.

Peter downed the last of his beer and, in a fierce motion, crushed the can flat and let it fall to the ground. As he left their company and moved slowly toward the girl, he could feel a hundred curious, hostile eyes following him.

The girl glanced up as he approached. Peter was surprised that she looked so young. Although he would learn later she was older, he guessed then that she could not be more than thirteen or fourteen. He was even more surprised that her eyes were so blue and troubled. Ignoring the questions that suddenly appeared there, Peter took her hand firmly in his own, silently pulled her to her feet, and headed for the path that led from the clearing toward the stream a short distance away. He was amazed that she did not resist.

Walking slowly through the camp with the girl behind him, Peter arrogantly returned the hard, animal stares now focused upon him as they had been upon the girl. Determinedly, the two moved past clusters of bodies passed out or sleeping on patches of grass, small groups of laughing, jeering men, and those coupled and hidden away beyond the ring of light from the campfire.

"You holding class somewhere, Professor?" sneered a husky male voice out of the shadows. "I want to learn how a real man does it!"

A roar of laughter filled the space around them. Peter, ignoring the challenge, did not break stride. He knew that taking such a prize from under their noses would not go unchallenged. But he did not know who would challenge his claim to her, or where, or when. Trying to appear relaxed, he tensed every nerve and muscle as his senses scanned the dark path ahead for what he was sure awaited them there. He had earned the nickname Professor because he had graduated from high school—most of the others had not—and because of the books that constantly accompanied him.

"You got a book with directions?" came another voice.

"H--- no, man!" cracked a third. "He's got a map so's he won't get lost!" Again there was laughter. Peter and the girl kept moving until at last they left the clearing and entered the path.

Suddenly their way was blocked by the rival club leader who had been turned away earlier by the girl.

24

"Where you takin' my dinner?" he snarled through thin, smiling lips as his eyes cautiously left Peter to look at the girl and then returned.

"What's it to you?" Peter answered his challenge.

The smile evaporated slowly as the man's eyes became wary slits under heavy brows. For a long moment he watched Peter. There was movement in the bushes. Peter could sense steel blades being unsheathed all around them. Battle lines were being formed. Peter hoped his own club was among them. He knew there would not be trouble as long as the girl remained the issue. The unspoken laws of the wild involving capture and possession would be respected, once his claim to her was proven. But it would be an entirely different matter if he did or said anything that would threaten club honor. He had to be careful.

Stepping forward, the man grabbed the girl's breast. Crying out in surprise and pain, she jerked away and moved behind Peter.

"That's what it's to me!" the man exclaimed loudly enough for all to hear as he looked with mock appreciation at his hand, held out for the unseen eyes around them to admire.

"She's mine, man," Peter stated flatly.

"Yeah?" barked the rival.

"Yeah," Peter answered.

For a long moment the two men stood toe to toe, each trying to intimidate the other with a stare. At last Peter could stand the tension no longer. Slowly and carefully he lit a cigarette, not taking his eyes off the man in front of him. The man's left eye was twitching, a clear sign that he, too, was feeling the pressure. At last he broke his stare and looked around, shifting his weight from one leg to the other and back again as though incredulous.

"Says who?" he demanded.

"Says her!" Peter felt the girl tense behind him and tighten her grip on his vest. The man turned his eyes upon the girl.

"Hey, b----! You his mama?" he spat at her.

Keeping his weight evenly distributed and on the balls of his feet, Peter held his breath for her answer. If she said no, then he would have to surrender her or fight. He could feel her shivering as she pressed against him. She did not answer.

"Hey! I'm talkin' to you, b----!" the man barked angrily. "Are you his mama or ain't you?"

Peter could feel the blood surging through a vein in his neck as his heart pounded out a frantic war beat. For a moment he was afraid the girl again would not answer. At last she spoke.

"Yes," she said softly.

Curses poured from the man's mouth as he once again eyed Peter. Then in a sign of resignation, he lifted his hands shoulder high, palms turned toward Peter, and began to back away.

"Later, man!" he said to Peter. "Later." His smile returned as he faded into the shadows. The sounds in the bushes now moved away from them. With a deep sigh of relief, Peter once again took the girl by the hand and they walked on.

With the expected challenge now behind him, Peter could turn his full attention to the girl. As he did so, a fierce, determined rage began to boil within him. It was not the girl who angered him as much as what she represented.

The light grew dim as they moved deeper into the forest. In a short time they found themselves near the rushing stream. It was dark and silent, except for faint noises from the camp and the splashing of water over rocks.

"Where are you taking me?" the girl asked in a tentative, frightened voice.

"Right here," Peter answered, his voice cold and harsh. His rage swelled out of control as he stared at her standing helplessly before him. The words tore from his constricted throat through clenched teeth. "What's your name, b----?"

The girl's gasp of shock did not escape him. Neither did the panic which suddenly flashed across her face.

"Susan," she answered at last, her voice trembling. "My name is Susan. What are you going to do?" She began to sob softly.

Her tears only added fuel to Peter's rage. He wanted her to know the same horror and agony he had felt when his father had held him pinned to the floor while his mother mercilessly switched the bottoms of his feet until they were ragged and bleeding.

"Shut up and take your clothes off!" he commanded heartlessly.

"Oh no, please don't! Dear God, please don't hurt me!" she begged pitifully and tried to step away. Her weeping now turned to desperate, sobbing gasps.

Grabbing a handful of hair, Peter jerked her back to stand in front of him, his face only an inch from hers.

"Take your clothes off, lady, or I'm going to take them off for you!" he spat at her.

Slowly the girl's hands moved to the top button of her shirt. She began undressing. Something inside Peter cried out for her to refuse, to fight back. But she did not.

Still crying hysterically, the girl was at last standing naked before him, her clothes piled in a heap at her feet. She kept her face turned away, her hands covering her eyes. She was shaking so hard she could hardly stand up.

Again the rage swelled in Peter as he felt no pleasure in her nakedness. In a fury, he forced her to lie down. Standing over her, he took out his knife. Without taking his eyes from the girl, he opened the knife and slashed the length of his right palm, just deep enough to break the skin. Satisfied, he returned the knife to its sheath and removed his belt with his left hand, while flexing his right to cover it with his own blood. Placing one end of the leather strap in the palm of his bloodied hand, he wrapped it around twice and closed his iron grip upon it. With the metal buckle dangling threateningly at the other end, Peter had created a deadly weapon. Seething with hatred, he lifted his arm, ready to bring that weapon down with full force upon the girl. But in that brief moment, the girl moved. Turning on her side, she pulled her knees up tight to her chest and buried her head in her arms. Her body was shaking violently as her gasping sobs turned to deep groans of anguish.

Looking at her, Peter saw himself as a young boy, lying naked on the living room floor in that same helpless position as his adopted mother and father beat him again and again. The memories of that night flashed in endless succession through his mind until at last he heard himself screaming for mercy out of his madness.

Slowly the memories began to fade. As the excruciating pain and panic subsided, Peter's mind began to clear. He became aware of the tree trunk in front of him, beaten and scarred, with pieces of torn bark hanging loose and lying on the ground. His heart was pounding madly and his body was drenched with sweat. The belt, still grasped firmly in his hand, was torn to shreds. The buckle was gone from the tattered end. His rage was spent. The nightmare had ended.

In the emptiness of extreme fatigue, Peter cried. Collapsing to his knees, he wrapped his aching arms around the ragged trunk of the tree and hung on as though he were once again a helpless child clinging desperately to a dog, a sister, a dream—anything that would make the nightmare end. For long moments he could not control his tears. But at last they too began to subside.

Then he heard it. A voice. Soft and gentle. And familiar—a voice he had heard many times as a child while alone and frightened. It was his real mother's voice. Singing.

"Jesus loves me, this I know . . . "

Closing his eyes, Peter listened intently. He could almost feel her arms around him as she held him in her lap, rocking and singing him to sleep. Over and over the voice sang. The same words. It was a song that brought him a sense of hope and peace. He wanted her voice never to stop, to go on singing to him forever.

"Are you all right?" whispered another voice nearby.

Suddenly remembering the girl, Peter was embarrassed and ashamed. He brushed away the tears and turned slowly to look at her. Every muscle ached from the effort. She was sitting upright, with legs tucked under her, clutching her clothes.

He did not know what to say. How to explain. To make her feel better. Everything was gone now—the rage, the nightmare, the fear and panic and madness, the voice and the peace it had brought. In their place was an emotional emptiness so deep Peter just wanted to go to sleep and never wake up. But there she sat. Looking at him. Alone and still frightened. He had to find some way to help her.

"Yes, I'm all right," he was able to say at last. "Why don't you get dressed?" Standing up slowly, he walked to a rock near the stream and sat down. Lighting a cigarette, he was too tired to drag his feet out of the water sloshing over them. He could hear Susan hurriedly putting her clothes on, her breathing frantic and shallow. The pain he felt now was for her.

After a moment he heard her approaching. Without looking, he knew she had stopped out of his reach. For a long moment there was silence. Then she spoke.

"Can I go now?" she asked awkwardly. He could tell she was still frightened and confused, as though not sure what to do next.

Peter sighed deeply. There was a part of him that wanted her to just go away and leave him alone. But he knew there was no place for her to go except back to the camp. And he knew what was waiting for her there.

"Yeah, you can leave now if you want to," he answered as he turned to look at her. "But I don't think that's such a good idea."

"Why not?" she asked suspiciously.

"Because some of the others are waiting for you."

There was a long silence as she thought this over. He sensed her returning panic as its full impact came upon her.

"You mean they are waiting to . . . to hurt me?" she blurted at last, her voice filled with fear once more.

"Yeah, that's what I mean," Peter answered softly.

"Oh no," she cried, sitting down hard where she stood. "What am I going to do?"

"You'll be all right if you stay with me," Peter told her after a moment. "I won't hurt you any more. I promise." He hoped she would believe him.

For a long time they did not speak, both lost in their own thoughts and the uncertainties of the moment. Peter was surprised when she moved to sit next to him.

"Why not?" she asked as she settled herself uncomfortably on the rock.

"Why not what?" Peter asked, not sure what she was asking.

"Why won't they bother me if I am with you?" She was still nervous. But at least her breathing had slowed and was more regular.

"Because they think I have made you my mama," Peter answered.

"Your mama?" she asked softly.

"My woman."

"Oh," she stated her understanding. Again there was a long silence. Peter was powerfully aware of her presence. He struggled for something to say. He did not often talk with women, particularly alone.

She was the first to speak. "Would you really have hurt me awhile ago?"

"Susan, I'm sorry about all that. I didn't really want to hurt you. Honest! It's just . . . well, I don't know. I guess I just went crazy." Peter pleaded for her to understand.

"But would you have?" she pressed.

"I don't know," he whispered. "I hope not."

Again there was an awkward silence. Peter did not dare to look at her. He had no idea what she was thinking. But his own thoughts left him weary and numb. Soon he felt her move closer.

"What am I going to do?" she whispered.

The desperation in her voice saddened Peter. He felt sorry for her. She was forced to turn for help and protection to the very man who only moments before was ready to beat her. It reminded him of his own childhood dependency upon his adopted parents. He knew well the emotional agony of having to trust one's life to the very person who could so easily destroy it.

"Please, Susan. I'll help you. I promise you'll be all right if you stay with me. And I'll take you home tomorrow," he pleaded once more. "Are you still afraid of me?"

"Not as much as of the others," she answered. "At least you didn't hurt me when you could have."

Again the pair lapsed into silence. Eventually they both relaxed and found some comfort in each other's presence. Peter's thoughts turned to the events of the next day. The bikers would travel en masse out of the mountains and through the many small towns along the return trip to home turf. Susan could ride with him. After they had spent the night together, Peter was sure the others would give them no trouble.

The ride out of the mountains was the grand finale of any biker happening, staged for the curious and hostile crowds they knew would gather along the way. It was an important part of the gathering, in that it was the only sure way to get the attention of a world too preoccupied with itself to notice or care. People like parades. Bikers liked to parade. Without a responsive world, the bikers' existence would have been meaningless. In reality, the bikers needed to be hated as much as the world needed to hate.

Two

Daylight the next morning found Peter and Susan huddled on a thick bed of leaves and grass under a tree. After they sat up talking most of the night, fatigue had at last overtaken them. Secure enough for the moment in each other's company, they had stretched out on the leaves and gone to sleep. As he slowly became aware of the cool morning moisture on his face, Peter was startled to find Susan snuggled close beside him, her head resting on his shoulder. He was more startled to find his arms wrapped tightly around her.

Being so close to her frightened Peter at first. It was not her body pressed against his that made him afraid. There had been other bodies the past couple of years. What frightened him most was the intimacy he felt with her at that moment. It felt good. Too good. It reminded him of things he was trying to forget. Fighting the urge to run and hide, he forced himself to relax and tentatively enjoy the moment— the feel of her so close beside him, the warmth of her breath on his neck, the smell of her hair lying in matted strands across his face.

In silence Peter watched the shadows of the passing night give way reluctantly to a new day. He was filled with an uncontrollable joy and reverence as the first edge of a bright yellow sun appeared through the trees on the mountaintop. Its light and warmth on his skin brought memories of other sunrises long ago—sunrises he had watched as a boy from his treetop perch near a river. Memories of a lonely, desperate child seeking acceptance from a world that had no place for him, love from people whose hearts and lives had no room for him.

Lost in his memories of other times and places, Peter was not aware that Susan was awake and watching him until she moved. Slowly and gently, her hand moved from his chest to the cross around his neck. Picking it up, she turned it toward her to look at it more closely.

Suddenly tense, Peter began to move away. He fully expected to see anger and disgust in her eyes. Instead, there was sensitive caring within their deep blueness as they searched his face curiously.

"Don't move," she whispered softly, and Peter left his arms around her, suddenly unsure of himself.

"Why do you wear this cross?" she asked a moment later, still holding it.

Peter thought for a moment. He was still trying to understand why she had not pushed him away. It amazed him that she could be so comfortable while he was so close and touching her.

"It's a symbol of hypocrisy," he muttered at last.

"I thought it was supposed to be a symbol of love," Susan observed.

"Yeah? Love for who?" Peter asked sharply.

"For us, silly!" she answered lightly, looking at him again. "God's love for all of us."

"God doesn't love," Peter blurted in response. "He only regrets!"

"Regrets what?" she asked, after a moment's thought.

"Creating us!" There was bitterness in his voice. "Wouldn't you regret creating people who turn out like me?"

"Oh, you don't really believe that, do you? You're not so bad!" She lay her head on his chest, not waiting for an answer.

Her question had taken him by surprise. Never before had anyone asked him what he believed. Even worse, no one had ever seemed to care.

"I don't know what I believe anymore," he said, picking up the cross to look at it himself. As he did, Susan saw the cut across his palm.

"What happened to your hand?" she asked, concerned, and took his hand to examine the wound more closely.

"I cut it."

"It looks terrible. Does it hurt?"

"No," he lied. Actually it was very sore. He could barely close it into a fist. But he hardly noticed the pain in the warmth of her attention. It felt so good to have someone care about him, to look at him with something other than contempt and hate. For a time he allowed himself to imagine what it would be like if the moment continued forever. But even as he imagined it, Peter knew it would not last. Susan, like all the other special women in his life, would soon be gone. Probably forever.

A rustling in the bushes along the path drove the couple apart. Startled, Peter was on his hands and knees in one swift movement, every sense scanning the forest around them. Suddenly aware once more of where they were and why, he carefully monitored the sounds until at last they stopped. Accompanied by sodden grunts and groans, a bleary-eyed, still-wasted biker from one of the other clubs began to relieve himself only a dozen feet from where they sat. The man was concentrating so hard on his task that he did not notice Peter and Susan and soon plodded back toward the camp.

Peter sighed deeply and began to relax once again. He looked at Susan. She appeared tired as she strained to see where the man had gone. The expression in her eyes only a moment before was gone, replaced now by fear. Their special precious moment together was also gone, swept away into life's treasured memories by the harsh realities of their situation. Once again Susan was a young woman in over her head. And Peter was what he was—a biker—an outcast, one of life's misfits caught between heaven and hell, a renegade saint. It made him want to vomit.

"Are you scared?" he asked.

"Yes," she said simply, without a moment's hesitation. She tried to smile, but failed.

Her answer hurt and angered Peter. It was not what he had wanted to hear.

"Didn't I tell you they wouldn't mess with you so long as you're with me?" he barked, regretting the words as soon as he said them. He watched through the window of her eyes as she withdrew into herself. In an instant she was gone, hidden behind an expressionless face.

Wounded and vulnerable, Peter got to his feet and lit a cigarette, his hands shaking with emotion. He took a deep drag and let the smoke out slowly, hoping to calm his ragged nerves. Eying Susan harshly and seeing a stranger, he once again became defensive and withdrew into his hard, uncaring shell. It would not take long to convince himself that he really did not care about Susan or about what she thought of him. Everything would be as before. Before they met. Before they had touched—and cared. Once again he would be safe, locked away in his world of arrogance and indifference, a world cold and empty of another's touch—a world he knew so well.

"So," he said at last, "what do you want to do?"

"I just want to go home." She answered lifelessly without looking at him.

"What about your parents? Will they let you come home?"

"Yes, I'm sure they will," she assured him. "They're probably worried sick by now."

Peter's stomach felt like a bottomless pit, sucking him into its depths. A part of him wanted Susan to go home where she belonged. Another part, desperate and grasping, did not want to let her go.

"All right then. If that's what you want, I'll take you. Come on!" Peter commanded and started toward the path back to camp. What she said next stopped him in his tracks.

"I don't even know your name." She was looking at him again.

"What the hell do you care?" he shot at her, unable to control the turmoil within him.

"I do care," she stated quietly.

"Like hell you do! The only thing you care about is getting out of here in the same condition you came in!" he stormed back.

Ignoring his outburst, Susan continued. "Will you tell me your name?"

Suddenly his anger was gone. "Peter," he sighed.

"That's a pretty name. I like it," she added, trying to smile again. For a moment their eyes met, then drifted apart.

"What about you, Peter? Do you have a family to go home to?"

"I've got a couple of brothers in the service," he heard himself saying. "But I don't see them much anymore. I guess it's just me."

"I wish you had a family to care about you, Peter," she said.

"Yeah, well, it really doesn't matter. I've been on my own too long. Besides, who wants to care about a low-life biker? Come on, let's get out of here."

Taking her by the hand, Peter pulled her to her feet and they moved quickly down the path toward camp. The many voices became more distinct as they neared the clearing. Peter stopped short of the camp while they were still hidden by the trees.

"Now listen to me! Stay close beside me. Until we get out of here, you are my mama. Don't even look at one of the others. Got it? And do whatever I say, no matter what. OK? And here, wear this." Peter removed the sleeveless jacket that bore his club's colors and helped Susan put it on over her shirt. By giving her his colors, he was announcing to the world that she was off limits to all others. But looking at her as the others would, Peter was not satisfied. She did not look like a mama.

"That's not good enough," he stated critically. "To play the part you've got to look the part. Take your bra off." For an instant Susan hesitated. There was just a hint of suspicion in her eyes. "Come on, d-----! We're not playing a game here. Just do it, OK?"

Her hesitancy gone, she quickly stripped off the vest and shirt. Removing her bra, she started to put her shirt back on.

"No, wait a minute," he commanded. "Just wear the vest and fasten the bottom three snaps."

Susan did as instructed and tucked her other clothes inside the vest. That did it. She looked like the other women in the camp. Peter was satisfied.

As they stepped out of the forest into the clearing, Peter pulled Susan close beside him and draped his arm possessively across her shoulders. Moving slowly, he led her through the curious and groggy crowd to his chopper near those of the others in his club. Peter could feel the bloodshot eyes as they moved from Susan to him and back again.

They entered the company of his own club without incident. Although there was not a man who would not have welcomed a chance to have Susan, Peter knew she would be safe among them. They would defend and protect her as they would a brother. Peter was a brother. She was his woman. That made her family.

Despite the fact that after two days of drinking, drugs, and very little sleep, tempers were short-fused, desires insatiable, and bodies nervous, the camp was too busy for conflict within itself. Preparations for departure were well underway by midmorning. With meticulous care, each man cleaned and polished his bike until it dazzled in the morning sunlight.

Once satisfied their bikes were ready, the men turned their attention to their own grooming. Dressed in boots and greasy blue jeans, and wearing their colors, they adorned themselves with an array of chains, armbands, medallions, helmets, and bandanas in an attempt to look as fierce and unkempt as possible. They were a shocking contrast to their bikes.

It was important that all the men and machines look their best for the final run of the weekend. After all, public images and reputations must be maintained if they were to retain the fear and respect so essential to a group's survival.

While the men busied themselves with themselves, some of the women began erecting the monument that would be left behind as a silent testimonial to the weekend presence of the bikers. It was a monument that would be talked about for days in the schools and cafes of nearby towns. All the empty liquor bottles and beer cans were piled in the middle of the clearing, finally towering high overhead. Then the flip-tops of beer cans were interlocked to form a long chain. Using nearby trees, the chain was stretched around the pile of beer cans several times to form a fence. Once completed, it was an impressive sight—a fitting monument to the lives it represented.

Like the others, Peter could feel the tension and excitement mounting as departure time grew near. This was to be the grand finale! It was really going to be something to see. Even more important, the residents in that part of the country would talk about it for years and most likely would be extra respectful the next time a small group of bikers happened along. Peter was excited. He could hardly wait.

At last the signal to start engines was given. What began as a grinding of ignitions and throttles soon became a thunderous roar of more than two hundred twelve-hundred-cubic-centimeter engines, all being revved at the same time. The noise could be heard for miles around. Peter knew this was an intentional signal to the local townsfolk and the state police stationed at the foot of the mountain that the pack was on the move.

Slowly the clubs began to form double lines, each club's members staying together in the pack. With Susan behind him, holding on tight, Peter moved his chopper in line with the others. As the procession made its way slowly down the mountain, Peter could see the line of bikers stretching out for more than a mile. It was an incredible sight!

At the foot of the mountain, at least thirty law enforcement vehicles were waiting, with twice as many uniformed officers lining the highway. Most were helmeted and armed with nightsticks, sidearms, and tear gas—to provide a peaceful escort out of the county.

Careful not to violate the speed limit, the chain of bikers moved steadily through the law. Peter could feel the cold, hard stares of nervous men hired to protect others from men like himself as he rode casually through them—knowing full well he was protected by the same law they were there to enforce. It was a confrontation between law and outlaw the bikers knew they would win.

Peter felt Susan's grip tighten as they entered the town. The main street down which they moved was lined with hundreds of onlookers turned out to witness the human spectacle. Occasionally a woman would express her disgust, especially toward the women, who rode defiantly behind the bikers as the men shouted out their curses.

Despite the catcalls and challenges issued by some of the town's young and reckless, Peter knew, from other such encounters, they were fairly safe as long as they kept moving. It would not be until they had broken into smaller groups along the way that they would be most threatened by rednecks and bands of high school boys out to prove their manhood.

Peter searched many of the faces lining the street as he followed the others. There was a time when he would have wanted to see friendliness and acceptance there. But he had convinced himself that it really did not matter what people thought of him.

Although there remained something in him that hated to be hated, he also found satisfaction and a sense of peace in the crowd's reaction. Rejection, he could handle; people's expectations, he could not. For it was always in another's expectations that Peter found his greatest weaknesses and inadequacies. And invariably his inadequacies were in areas that seemed to bring the greatest grief and suffering to those he cared most about.

A part of Peter envied the people standing along the street. Their lives seemed so simple, so sane—such a contrast to his own. At the very least, they had one another—friends and family. He fantasized what it must be like to be one of them, standing there indignant, frightened, righteous enough to band together in large numbers to drive the wolves away from the sheep and the leper from the well.

But somewhere in his mind, Peter believed he would never be like them. He would always be different. He was bad. There was no place for him in their world.

These and a thousand similar thoughts played through his mind as the town limits came into view. As the long line of bikers left the town and entered the flow of traffic on the highway, Peter felt exhilarated, victorious. Once again he had faced his judge and jury and walked away a free man, believing even more in who he thought he was. He felt justified.

As the pack headed south along the highway, small groups of bikers broke away at exits along the way, each club moving toward its own destination. The weekend was over, and so was the truce that had made it possible. Defense of territorial claims would once again become the barrier between the clubs until the next happening.

Many of them, Peter knew, would not return. Some would be in prison, others dead. Some might even break away from their club and its self-destructive life-style to seek a new life—out there . . . somewhere. Maybe Peter would be one of them.

Three

Susan's hometown was less than an hour's ride from the site of the rock concert. Despite the protests of several club members, Peter decided to take her home alone. Although he knew a lone rider was an easy target, he also knew they had a better chance of avoiding unwanted attention if they were alone. He could handle the occasional civic-minded motorist who would try to run him off the road. It was the pickup trucks loaded with men out to defend their homes and families from a pestilence of motorized vermin that he most wanted to avoid.

Leaving the rest of his club waiting at a bar along the highway, Peter and Susan rode silently along a winding country road until her hometown came into view. Peter noticed the sign at the city limits that welcomed him to Warrior Country, Home of the 1967 State Champions. Nor did he miss the warning painted in sprawling, hand-written letters across the bottom of the sign: "If you don't like it, get the h--- out!"

Ignoring the few people who stopped to stare at them, Peter followed Susan's directions until they neared her house. Knowing the reaction of her parents if they saw their daughter ride up on a motorcycle with her arms wrapped around a biker, Peter stopped on a side street several blocks away. She could walk the final distance.

Peter let the bike idle while Susan climbed off. She took a brush from her handbag and began to brush her windblown hair.

"Thanks for bringing me home, Peter," she said between painful strokes.

"Sure, Bambino," he answered from behind his dark glasses.

She stopped brushing to smile at him.

"Bambino? What's a bambino?" she laughed.

"You're a bambino!"

After exchanging addresses and phone numbers, the two promised to stay in touch. Then it was time to part. Stepping close, Susan hugged him long and hard before turning on her heel and walking away. It was all Peter could do to let her go.

"Hey you!" he called after her. She stopped and looked back. She was crying. He had not expected that. For a moment he could not speak.

"What?" she said after a moment.

"You call me if you ever need me," Peter told her, trying desperately to keep his voice steady. "I'm only a phone call away. Right?"

"I will," she promised, and with that she was gone.

It had been harder to leave Susan than he had imagined. He realized his attraction to her went a great deal deeper than a chance encounter at a rock concert.

Once out of the city limits Peter opened the throttle and rode at breakneck speed through the countryside on his way back . . . back to what? He knew what he was leaving, but where was he going? Back to the way it was before he had met Susan? Somehow that did not seem possible. Something had changed . . . or maybe everything had changed. Peter's mind burned with confusion; his heart ached with emptiness and loneliness. He was glad the wind was whipping against his face, drying the tears as fast as they appeared.

• • •

Peter and Susan did stay in touch—mostly by letter, but occasionally by phone. She was welcomed back into her family after her weekend with the bikers and seemed to get along better with her parents. In time she was able to finish high school, and she told Peter she planned to enter a broadcasting school to become a disc jockey.

Peter was proud of her, and he told her so on their occasional visits when he was in the area. Knowing the trouble it could cause if her parents knew about him, Peter would stop at a nearby phone booth to call, and Susan would meet him at a hamburger shack on the edge of town. They would visit for hours.

Susan took a job as a waitress to earn the money she would need for broadcasting school. It was then that Peter lost track of her. There were no more letters and no more phone calls. Busy with his own day-to-day survival, Peter thought nothing of it at first. He was sure she would write soon. But months passed and still no letters came. One morning Peter woke up knowing something was wrong. Worried now, he had to see her.

Back in her hometown, he stopped at the usual phone booth and dialed the number. After what seemed an eternity, her mother's voice answered.

"Is Susan home?" he asked cautiously.

There was a long pause. Peter could hear the woman's heavy breathing.

"Who wants to know?" she asked suddenly, her voice harsh and bitter.

"I'm a friend of hers," Peter stalled, trying to think of a name he could use. For a second he was afraid the woman would hang up. But she didn't.

"A friend, huh?" she queried. "Well, you must not be such a d--- good friend is all I can say! Everybody around here knows she ran off with that man from the restaurant. About four months ago now, I guess. She hasn't bothered to write or phone. Her father and I don't know where she is now. Or who she's with. Or what she's doing. And I just don't care anymore!" The woman began to cry softly. "Now please, just leave us alone."

The phone clicked. For a long time Peter stood in the booth with the phone still pushed hard against his ear, stunned by what the woman had said. Susan gone? Ran off with some guy? He couldn't believe it! She was working to pay her way through broadcasting school. She couldn't be gone!

Desperately, his mind sought reasons to disbelieve the woman. She was lying! But then, why would Susan's mother want to lie about something like that? He would have to find out for himself.

Grabbing the phone book, Peter tore at the yellow pages to find the listing for restaurants. Susan had mentioned the name in one of her letters. He was sure he would recognize it when he saw it. Racing his finger down the list, he found it: The Tackle Box—Restaurant and Lounge. That's the one, he thought to himself as he tore the page from the book and tucked it in his pocket. A moment later he was on his way.

At a gas station down the street from the restaurant, he parked his bike and took some clothes out of the bedroll strapped to the rear seat. In the restroom, he stripped off his colors, denims, boots, and chains, washed his face and hands quickly, and clothed himself in clean, though sadly wrinkled, sport shirt and blue jeans. He added a pair of sneakers and took a final glance in the mirror. Then he pulled his shoulder-length hair into a pony tail, twisted it several turns, and tucked it under a baseball cap he kept for special occasions—occasions when he needed to look straight. Like now.

When he arrived at the restaurant, Peter looked like some high school kid who had been out joy-riding. He parked his bike near the entrance, pointing it in the direction of most immediate escape, and took a deep breath in an attempt to calm himself. He entered and immediately recognized the place for what it was—a fast-food joint with attached bar as cover for illicit activities. He had seen many such places and had even helped establish a couple. Several people were huddled around a pool table in a dimly lighted back room. The juke box was bellowing out a mournful country melody that both teased and taunted him, making him more edgy. The dining room was empty except for a couple at a table in the far corner. A man was standing at the cash register.

"Excuse me, sir?" Peter said as he approached.

"Yes, can I help you?" the man answered without looking up.

What a fool, Peter thought as he watched the man carelessly counting money. At another time and place, and under different circumstances, Peter would have taken it all, right from under the man's nose. But he had other business today.

"Can you tell me if Susan is working tonight?"

"Susan?" the man's head shot up.

"Yes, sir. Is she working tonight? It's really important that I talk with her. It'll only take a second."

The man, suddenly tense and suspicious, stared hard at Peter, his eyes seeming to search for something. He finally spoke. "You must not be from around here."

"Why do you say that?" Peter countered, fighting the impatient anger beginning to swell inside him. He wanted answers, not games. He was tempted to jerk the man up short and tell him so.

"Everybody around here knows Susan ran off with my cook about—oh let's see . . . guess it's been three, four months ago now. They emptied the cash register on their way. That's why!"

Apparently Susan *had* left her job and gone off with this guy. But why? Peter had to find out.

"You're right. I'm not from around here. I'm Susan's brother. We haven't seen each other in a long time," he lied. "It's very important that I find her. Can you tell me where they went?"

"I didn't know Susan had a brother!" the man exclaimed, looking at Peter with new curiosity. "She never mentioned one to me."

"Well, trust me, she does! And I'm it. Please, can you tell me where she went?" There was impatience in his voice now.

"Last I heard, they were in Texas somewhere. Houston, maybe. Or Dallas. H--- man, I don't know! If I did, they'd both be in jail!"

"Who does know?" Peter pressed urgently. "Somebody here must have known her and talked with her some. Maybe a friend?"

"Hey, wait a minute. Maybe Nancy knows something. She and Susan used to hang around a lot together. Why don't you have a seat over there at one of those tables while I go get her. She's working the bar tonight."

At last he was getting somewhere. Excited now, Peter walked over to a corner booth where he could sit with his back to the wall and have a full view of everything.

After a few moments a young woman about Susan's age, Peter guessed, came out of the back room, wiping her hands on a towel. With little introduction, Peter told her the same story he had told the restaurant manager. She, too, seemed confused to hear that Susan had a brother. Brushing off her doubts, Peter spoke quickly and urgently.

"Can you tell me where she is?" he pleaded.

"Are you the heat?" she asked suspiciously.

"No, I'm not a cop!" Peter reassured her.

"Well, if you are, Susan didn't do anything wrong. She didn't take that money. Johnny did that!" Her tone was emphatic.

45

"That's not why I'm here," he explained again. "I couldn't care less about the money. I'm her brother, like I told you, and it's very important that I find her."

As she listened, the woman seemed to relax. In place of suspicion there was concerned urgency. She lit a cigarette and began telling the story.

She and Susan had been good friends ever since high school. It was she who had gotten Susan the job in the restaurant. Everything was going fine until Johnny, the new cook, was hired. Susan was living with her parents, saving her money, and making plans to enter broadcasting school. But then she began to go out with Johnny. They seemed to hit it off from the first meeting. That's when Susan began to change.

"What do you mean, *change?*" Peter pressed the woman as she paused to light another cigarette.

"Susan began showing up late for work," Nancy went on. "That wasn't like her. She was always so prompt. Then she started losing weight. And she was tired all the time. Sometimes there were bruises on her arms and around her wrists."

"What from?" Peter demanded. He did not like what he was hearing.

"I don't know," Nancy answered. "But I have my suspicions. I think Johnny turned her on to drugs."

"D---!" Peter exploded, burning with anger.

"Then one day she didn't show up for work at all. I called her house, but they didn't know where she was either. I was really worried about her. Then she called a couple days later and told me she and Johnny were going to get married in his hometown. Somewhere in Texas. She wanted me to send her last paycheck to her."

"Where?" Peter demanded impatiently.

"Dallas," she answered.

Peter made a move to leave, but she grabbed him by the arm and pulled him back into the booth.

"Wait a minute. That's not all! They're in Houston now. And Susan is in trouble. Big trouble! I got a letter from her a couple of weeks ago. It's here in my purse somewhere."

"Well, find it!" Peter was almost frantic. "Let me see it."

When she had unearthed the letter, he grabbed it from her hand and began to read. Susan must have been crying as she wrote. There were what looked like tear stains on the page.

Dear Nancy,

Johnny isn't anything like I thought he was. He's a criminal, Nancy! He's wanted by the FBI. I just found out! We've been running from the law ever since we left. And his name is not Johnny!

I thought it would be different after the baby came. But it's only worse! He hurts me a lot. I'm so afraid he's going to hurt the baby. He stays stoned all the time.

He said a little while ago that he can't work because of the law being after him and all. So he said I was going to have to make some money for us. I'm so scared, Nancy! He says he'll kill me if I try to leave. And he will! I know he will!

I've got to hurry and get this in the mail before he gets back. He said he was bringing some friends for me to meet. What am I going to do?

Peter was in a blind rage by the time he finished the letter. It had been a long time since he had wanted to kill. But he wanted to at that moment. He stuffed the letter in his pocket and raced from the restaurant without another word.

Like a madman, Peter rode straight through two days and nights to reach Houston. Once there, it did not take him long to locate the motel at the return address on the letter.

Parking his bike near No. 17, he shook the fatigue out of his body. He did not know what to expect. Or even if they were still there. But if they were, he wanted to be ready. With heart pounding, he knocked and waited. He had to knock several times before at last he heard Susan's voice on the other side. She sounded scared.

"Who's there?"

"It's me, Bambino. Let me in!" he exclaimed.

"Oh my G--!" he heard her gasp. "Peter! Peter, I can't believe it's you!"

The woman who opened the door was not the same girl Peter remembered. Her hair was stringy, and she looked thin and frail. There were bruises on her face and hands.

"Oh, Peter! I can't believe you're here!" she sobbed again and again as she clung to him. "I thought it was another one of his friends."

Peter closed the door and just stood holding her for a long time. She cried on and on.

The room was bare except for a couch. Susan explained later that "Johnny" had sold the motel furniture, since they had no source of income.

After a while Susan was able to loosen her grip and Peter went into the kitchen. Opening the refrigerator, he saw it contained only a bottle of ketchup, a half loaf of bread, a small package of cheese, and two six-packs of beer. Taking a beer, he tore the top off and drank long from the can.

The fury he had felt two days ago when he left on his journey returned now with frightening force. Continuing his search, he discovered there was nothing in the cupboards.

"The b------!" he muttered to himself.

Entering the bedroom, Peter saw a small bundle lying on the floor in the corner. It was the baby. Moving carefully so as not to awaken it, he leaned over to look. He could see Susan in its sleeping face. And someone else.

"This his baby?" he asked the woman now standing behind him.

"I think so," she answered. Her voice sounded strange.

Swallowing hard, Peter fought the tears of rage and hurt swelling inside. The storm within him blazed for long minutes before he could speak again.

"Get your things together," he ordered.

"What are you going to do, Peter? He'll be back soon!" she exclaimed.

"Don't worry, Bambino. Just get your things together and be ready to leave. When we hear him coming, I want you to stay here in the bedroom with the baby until I come for you. And keep the door shut! You hear?"

Nervously the young woman began collecting things and placing them in what looked like an old diaper bag. They talked while she went about her chore. It did not take long because there was not much.

An hour or so later they heard a pickup truck drive up to the door.

"That's him, Peter!" she cried out in a panic.

"Was he bringing anyone home with him?"

"Not this time, I don't think," she answered as she pulled the bedroom door closed behind her.

With Susan and the baby locked safely in the bedroom, Peter quickly moved behind the front door. He could hear the key scraping in the lock as he took out his knife and made a swift, shallow cut along the palm of his right hand. He let the pain feed his already boiling rage.

Then the door opened. Amid a string of curses, a man's head appeared, and Peter uncoiled with the force of pent-up hate. His fist smashed into the man's face, sending him sprawling against the wall. As if possessed, Peter pounced, his fists pounding out his fury. Again and again he struck. Memories of endless hours of childhood beatings flooded back into his mind, adding fuel to his madness. In a frenzy, he continued long after all resistance was gone.

At last his rage subsided. The man was lying in a pool of his own blood. Peter could not tell whether he was still breathing. He really didn't care. To this day he does not know whether the man survived.

Peter took the man's wallet and tucked Susan's small bag of belongings into his bedroll. He placed Susan and the baby behind him on the bike, and they began the long trip back.

In time Susan was able to find a job, rent her own apartment, and start a new life in a town near enough to her parents and friends so she could visit regularly. Although she never made it to broadcasting school, she later married, now has three children, and seems happy. And not once since that night has she heard from "Johnny."

Four

Christmas—a time of going home; a time of returning, of reunion with loved ones; a time for belonging to someone, somewhere. So for the first time, Peter went home on Christmas Eve.

Parking his bike off the dirt road at the top of the hill behind his adopted parents' house, he buried himself in the tall grass. Here he had a clear view of the house, the street in front of it packed with cars, the back porch, the yard filled with light.

Not so long ago it had been his home. He once had a place there. There might even have been a time when he belonged there. But no more. Now he was as unwelcome there as in any other house on the block. Maybe even more so.

Peter did not know what had brought him back. He had promised himself he would never return. Maybe it was the aloneness he felt after the other bikers had gone off for the holiday. Or maybe it was because he had nowhere else to go.

The house was aglow with lights and filled with laughing, cheerful people. Some of them Peter recognized as friends of the family. Occasionally he could hear his adopted mother's high, long laugh or catch a glimpse of one of his brothers among the others inside. They were on leave from the service. How Peter wished he could be with his brothers again.

Soon a small group left the house and moved slowly up the street, singing carols. They stopped and sang in front of each house until the door opened and its occupants stepped out to wish them a Merry Christmas. From his spot on the hill, Peter could hear every word. Their voices echoed through the valley sharp and clear.

For a moment he pretended he was there among them, snuggled in the warmth of their company, lifting his voice with theirs to spread the joyous message of love, hope, and goodwill. He even tried to sing with them, his voice raspy and choked with emotion. Hearing his own voice was like sitting close to a campfire on a bitterly cold night when the wind shifts just enough to push the heat in radiating waves around his body. The momentary pleasure of its warmth only reminded him of the cold emptiness all around him. He ached. And with the ache came tears of bitterness and despair.

Terribly depressed, he could stand it no longer. He returned to his bike and rode toward town. Feeling the power of the machine he controlled, a reckless abandon seized him. Mindlessly, he tore through a nearby neighborhood in a whirlwind of vandalism, slashing tires and throwing rocks through the windows of dark, deserted houses. Filled with the irresponsibility that comes when no one else cares, he gave no thought to what might happen.

Having no response from his destructive sweep through the neighborhood, Peter became angry and raced off down the main street. Still seething, he saw the church with its crowded parking lot only a short distance ahead. Without thinking, he pulled off the street and stopped. The front door was open wide. He could see the backs of the people packed inside, celebrating a midnight Christmas service.

For a long time he sat on his bike outside, watching the priest and choir lead the congregation in worship and singing carols. The altar was buried in beautiful poinsettias. The heavy wooden cross hanging above cast shadows on the wall, giving the effect of three crosses in silhouette. Peter was mesmerized by the sight, remembering other times long ago when he had sought refuge in an empty church and found peace there. Once again, he felt irresistibly drawn to the altar. He wanted to sit in the shadow of the cross, to know once more the peace it offered.

Lost in his own desperate need, Peter forgot the people in the church. Until they began to sing again. It was in the midst of "O Come, All Ye Faithful" that the scene before him faded into a more powerful and compelling vision . . . In his mind, he revved the bike's engine until it became a roar drowning out the haunting music. He imagined releasing the clutch, riding through the open door of the church and down the aisle to the altar, scattering people in every direction. He saw the angry man-child stare insolently at the priest, dressed in radiant eucharistic vestments. For a moment his purpose wavered as he saw only sadness in the man's eyes. But then the anger surged once more.

"Where the h--- were you when I needed you?" he heard himself scream at the priest. "Where are you now? Why are you lying to these people? You're not real! You're just a big, stinking joke!"

He raised his arm defiantly in an obscene gesture, turned his bike, and sped out of the church. . . .

Slowly the vision began to fade. It took several moments for Peter's eyes to focus once again on the scene of worship in the church. He was shaking in miserable rage. Suddenly he had to get away. Anywhere! Away from people, from sights and sounds and feelings and memories. Away from the child crying pitifully within him.

Stopped at a traffic signal, Peter noticed a police car in another lane. Bending over, he picked up a sizable rock and threw it. He heard the glass shatter before he heard the siren. The chase was on!

For a full fifteen minutes Peter led the officers on a wild ride through the back alleys and remote areas of town. Soon the patrol car was joined by others and Peter had to cut through vacant lots several times to avoid roadblocks. At the last intersection before the street ended at the beach, he revved his bike, jumped the curb, and raced onto the beach where the cars could not follow. The sirens slowly faded in the distance.

Peter rode for several miles on the hard-packed sand near the surf's edge. As the adrenalin subsided and he began to relax, he became aware of the pounding surf and the cold mist on his face—and that his anger was gone. In its place was the panic children feel when they suddenly become aware they have lost their parents in a crowd.

Desperate to know someone cared, Peter rode to a phone booth and called Susan. She was his only hope. There was no answer.

Deeply depressed once more, he stopped on a freeway overpass. High above the road below, he watched the cars streak by on their way to somewhere from somewhere until their tail lights became blurs in the distance. He wondered about the people in those cars—who they were, where they were going, whether they were happy. Finally he decided to get it over with. He climbed over the guard rail and prepared to jump. He stood there for a long time, waiting for someone in one of the passing cars to notice him and stop. No one did.

Helpless against his own feelings, he returned to his bike and made his way slowly back to his place on the hill overlooking his adopted home. Taking some marijuana and a pint of whiskey from his bedroll, he settled himself once more among the weeds. He would spend his Christmas alone, trying to make the pain go away.

Despite all Peter's efforts to drug himself into unconsciousness, sleep would not come. His mind raced on. Thoughts. Thousands of thoughts. Each demanding attention. He pursued them all and, by morning, found himself right back where he had started.

There were no answers. There never were. Just questions, doubts, fears. Despite his distrust of people, Peter was overwhelmed by a need to be near others, to have someone look at him and see him. Like the priest last night. Maybe if he went back to the church. . . .

It did not take long to get there. The sign in the yard indicated the Christmas Day service was scheduled to start at eleven. He was a little early. But he did not mind. Stepping cautiously through the heavy front door, Peter sat down in the corner of the last pew. He had made no effort to clean up or change clothes. He came just as he was.

At last the church began to fill with people. Peter watched quietly as the well-ordered families filed into the pews, each claiming its rightful place among the others. They were dressed in their holiday best, their hair combed and precisely in place. Seeing their neatness made him painfully aware of his own appearance. He was a freak, something that had crawled out of a wasteland to find itself in a place where it did not belong. But he dared not get up to leave for fear of attracting attention. He wished he were invisible.

No one sat near him. Though the church was crowded, the seats around him were left unclaimed throughout the service. Those in the congregation who became aware of his presence carefully ignored him, presuming that someone else, perhaps the ushers, would keep an eye on him. He was a renegade. A wolf among sheep. Wild, untamed, untouchable.

Normally that realization would have brought Peter great satisfaction. But on this day it brought him only pain. He did not want to be different. Not today. Not at Christmas!

Peter relaxed a bit as the service began. The first part of the liturgy concluded, the priest climbed into the pulpit to preach. For a moment Peter wanted to bolt. He could not stand the thought of someone standing up and telling him and everyone else how bad he was. He knew that already. He had heard it all from his parents. But he stayed.

After a few minutes, he realized, to his amazement, the priest was not talking about how sinful Peter was or reminding him that the wages of sin were death. Nor was the sermon an elaborate attempt to make him feel guilty for being human. Instead, it was in the form of a story—a story about a family long ago that had journeyed to a foreign place where their child was born. And how the shepherds and wise men came to adore the child, knowing he was the Messiah. It was a familiar story, one Peter had heard many times. But it had never been told like this! It was as though he were hearing it for the first time.

It was such a simple story—about a simple child who grew to become a simple man whose purpose was so simple and yet so profound! Even more startling was the fact that this man Jesus had been a real man, a real person just like Peter, or anyone else, for that matter.

This was a new and strange awareness for Peter. He had always believed Jesus was more God than man, above the trials and temptations of mortals, not subject to the same grief, suffering, and labor. But the more he listened to the priest's description of the Christmas event and its impact upon the world, the more his concept was challenged as to who and what this Jesus of Nazareth was all about.

Peter wanted to know more. He wanted to get to know this man Jesus personally. Maybe they had more in common than he had thought or could even imagine.

At last the sermon ended. It was followed by the offering. The priest had reminded Peter that Jesus had said it was better to give than to receive. Then he realized he had nothing to give. He had no money with him. As usual, he was inadequate.

Desperate, he tried to think of something to give in return for the few moments of peace and the personal challenge that had come to him during the sermon. Finally he took a pencil and a card from the back of the pew in front of him. For a long moment the pencil remained unmoved, poised above the card. His mind was filled with the Christmas message. Out of its churning possibilities came a single thought: *There is no meaning apart from God.* Then he began to write:

Consider the moon and its wondrous light;
Our only hope against eternal night.

It lights the night when no other can;
A steady companion to a lonely man.
It has a place in each love confessed;
An inspiration to a heart so blessed!
It fills the eyes with ephemeral glow,
And makes anxious time move ever so slow.
An immortal light in mortal sight;
Majestic ruler of eternal night.
But what would it be if not for its light?
A world of stone—cold and alone!
But with its light, a world of dreams
Warming each life with its golden beams.
There is no other in time or place
That can compare with its radiant face!
Having considered its beauty, its majesty, and power
Upon even the lowliest of earthly flower
I pause to ask you, as ask I must
What is the source of its perpetual light?

Since the church was so large, some time had passed before the usher with the offering plate hesitated near Peter, apparently wondering whether to hand it to him. Seeing the plate, Peter reached for it, placed the card in it, and returned it to the surprised and curious man. Having no money, Peter had offered the only thing he had to give—himself! Not completely—only a part. But an important part. For a very brief moment, Peter had opened his heart and mind to a living, redemptive Christ.

The service continued with the eucharistic prayers as the priest prepared the Sacrament and the congregation for Communion. Peter followed those preparations with a sense of peace he had not known for a very long time.

When it was time to walk to the altar rail and kneel with the others, Peter felt suddenly overwhelmed with self-consciousness. How desperately at that moment he wished he could look and talk and live like other people. How he wished he were wearing something other than dirty jeans and boots. He did not want to attract attention, be different from everyone else. Unless he were like the others, he thought, he had no right to share Communion with them. He was sure his participation in the Eucharist would only depreciate its importance in the minds of the faithful who had gone before him. How could they share the same table? Even more significant, how could God love them equally?

Fighting the urge to run and hide, Peter somehow found himself kneeling at the rail. After receiving the Sacrament, he was shocked to feel the priest's hand rest for a moment on his shoulder. Then it was gone. But the effect of being touched would remain—for the rest of his life. Slowly, with eyes on the floor and a heart filled with an unimagined joy, Peter returned to his seat.

The service ended a few minutes later. The priest gave his blessing to the congregation and urged the people to go in peace to love and serve the Lord. What did those words mean? Peter wondered.

When the clerical procession had left the church, Peter got to his feet immediately. He hurried past the priest waiting just outside the door and strode quickly to his bike, parked arrogantly at the curb directly in front of the church. Once again secure in his own world, he sat and watched the mass of people pour out of the building and across the lawn to the parish hall. Although he did not want to join them, neither did he want to leave. He wanted to think—about the story the priest had told about this man Jesus, about everything he had experienced during the service. Most of all, he wanted to think about the hand that had rested for a moment upon his shoulder.

Lost in thought, he suddenly sensed another's presence. Jerking his head up, he found himself looking into the eyes of the old priest. For an instant he was frightened by the gentleness and caring he saw there.

"What is bothering you, son?" the priest asked softly.

"Nuthin'," Peter answered defensively.

"You came to the service. Why?" the old man pressed.

The question caught Peter by surprise. He did not know what to say. So he decided to tell the truth. "Maybe I had nowhere else to go."

"Neither did I," said the priest. "I'm glad you came!"

"Sure you are!" Peter blurted. "You and everybody else. Right?"

"No, not everybody. Me. *I'm* glad you came," the old man answered calmly, still looking at Peter. "Are you a Christian?"

"H---, man! Do I look like a Christian?" Suddenly Peter was nervous and frightened.

"I don't know," answered the priest. "I don't really know what a Christian looks like. But I imagine you look a great deal as our Lord must have looked to the people of his time. A little out of place, maybe?"

"Yeah, out of place! That's me," snapped Peter.

"Does that cross you are wearing mean anything special to you?" the priest asked, ignoring Peter's ill temper.

Peter had forgotten about the cross around his neck. Without thinking, he reached up to touch it. For a moment he did not speak.

"Yeah," he answered finally. "It's a symbol."

"Of what?"

Peter was tempted to tell him it was none of his business. "Hope, for some; hypocrisy, for others!"

"And which does it represent for you?"

"Hypocrisy, man! Pure hypocrisy," Peter spat bitterly. "The church is full of hypocrites!"

"Yes, it is," the priest agreed kindly. "Can you think of a better place for them to be?"

The question had the same effect as a dash of cold water in the face. It got Peter's attention and held it. He had never thought about it like that before. The question teased his mind. He did not know what to answer.

"I've got to split, man!" he yelled instead. The old man was making him very uncomfortable. Peter liked him. That was frightening. He also liked what the priest was saying. Hurriedly, he began making preparations to leave.

"Before you go, son, there is a story I would like to share with you." The priest gently grasped Peter's arm. His grip was surprisingly firm.

Peter looked at the priest. There was a light in his eyes as he began the story:

An old man was sitting alone in his study one cold, wintry night. Suddenly he noticed a pecking at the window. Curious, the old man rose from his chair, went to the window, and opened it. There, outside in the freezing snow and ice, was a small bird. The man had compassion for the bird and thought what a wonderful companion it would make. He also knew the bird would not survive the night outside. Desperately, he tried everything he could think of to entice the bird into the warmth and security of the study, where it would find food, rest, and continued life. The darkness beyond the study window would bring only death. But the bird did not understand what the man was trying to do. It refused to enter. At last, in despair, the old man closed the window and returned to his chair by the fire, leaving the bird to suffer and die outside in the cold. His heart aching with grief and sadness, the old man thought to himself, "If only I were a bird, I could show that bird the way into the study and that it need not be afraid. Maybe if I were a bird, I could show it how to escape the death that awaits it in the darkness outside and lead it to a new life in the world beyond the study window.

Despite himself, Peter was listening intently, his mind expanding to absorb the many possible meanings.

The priest watched him for a moment before he spoke again. "God loves you so much, son, that he sent his Son to show you the way."

That got to Peter. It was more than he could handle. The only way he had been able to survive this long, he had convinced himself, was by believing no one cared.

"B--- s---!" he shouted as he jump-started the bike and raced its engine.

"Think about it," the old man added before releasing his grip on Peter's arm.

Covering his eyes with his sunglasses, Peter stared defiantly at the priest, then, without a word, raced off down the street.

Peter did not think about the story, as the priest had suggested. He went out and got drunk. It was the only way to quiet the echoes. Yet now, hardly a day passes that he is not reminded in one way or another that God loves him so much that he sent his Son to show him the way.

Five

It was the usual Saturday night. Like a swarm of hungry locusts, the crowd of festive diners had swamped the beach-front restaurant most of the evening. Since opening for dinner at five o'clock, the waitresses, cooks, and busboys had been working feverishly to feed one eager party after another. Now past midnight, only the ravages of a satisfied clientele remained.

Sitting alone in the now silent and dark piano bar filled with echoes from the evening, Peter critically surveyed the room full of tables piled high with dirty dishes. He was tired. And his head hurt. He had not slept well in months—not since talking with the priest. A restlessness unlike anything he had ever experienced had taken hold of him. He could not explain it. But it was driving him crazy.

Sighing deeply, he lit a cigarette and let his eyes move from the chaos in the room to the long stretch of beach visible through the large picture window that took up one entire wall of the lounge. As always, the sight thrilled him as some unexplainable urge lured him irresistibly to the shore.

He loved the bright full moon reflecting off the endless expanse of water and the line of white water that stretched the length of the beach as wave after wave cascaded across its hard-packed sands and jetties. He liked to think of this as the center of the universe—the point at which the earth, the sea, and sky all met. He imagined himself important enough to have a place beside its thriving life.

How many hours had he spent on that beach, he wondered. How many nights had he spent trying to keep warm among the rocks under the pier. He had gotten to know the beach well during those days. It had become his home. For a moment he allowed his mind to drift back two years to the day Buck had found him there, looking through the garbage cans for something to eat. Sick and exhausted, he had been rescued by Buck's group of bikers. It was Buck who had taken him in, given him something to eat and a place to stay. He was the closest thing to a friend Peter had, except for Susan.

It was Buck who had helped him get the job in the restaurant. And what a job—Peter found that even though he was frequently absent after he had joined the Saints, they were only too glad when he returned. Apparently good help was hard to find.

It was a miracle he had even been hired, Peter remembered. In the same T-shirt, blue jeans, and tennis shoes he had been wearing for weeks, and showing the obvious effects of living without food, shelter, or personal care, he had timidly entered the front door of the restaurant and asked the desk clerk if he could interview for the job. With a not surprising look of contempt, the well-kept clerk eventually went off to find the manager. Peter waited self-consciously in the lobby, and in a few moments, a woman who identified herself as the assistant manager appeared.

The interview was short, he remembered. He had given the woman his name and social-security number, admitted he had no experience, but lied about his age and address. He was hired on the spot. Lunch was to be served in an hour and the woman was desperate for busboys.

Taking Peter to the back room, the woman had outfitted him in a white shirt, black bow tie, cummerbund, and white jacket. He was told to buy himself a pair of black slacks and black shoes as soon as he could. In the meantime, his blue jeans and tennis shoes would have to do. Taking a large comb from her purse, the woman then carefully combed his hair.

Finally tailored to her satisfaction, he was taken into the kitchen to be introduced to the head cook, and where, much to his surprise and relief, the woman instructed him to tell the cook what he wanted to eat. Overwhelmed and self-conscious with the unfamiliar attention, Peter could not think of anything to order but a hamburger and Coke. He was told that his salary would consist of one dollar per hour, two hot meals per shift, and 5 percent of whatever his waitress made in tips each day.

Once again Peter felt the surge of joy and excitement of that day not so long ago. To have food, a job, and money after being so desperate! Just as a lot is little to those who have everything, a little is a lot to those who have nothing. To Peter it was a lot! He had felt like the luckiest man in the world.

For a long time Peter sat at the restaurant table, lost in the memory of that day. Then slowly another memory began pushing its way into his thoughts.

He had just completed his first week on the job. Although he associated with the bikers who had rescued him, he had not as yet been invited to join their ranks. The result was that he continued to sleep under the pier. But two hot meals a day had restored his health and strength. Keeping his money in an old sock tied to his belt and nestled snugly in his jeans pocket, even his confidence was beginning to return.

Thinking how fortunate he was, on that particular night Peter had made his way slowly down the street in and out of the shadows of street lights too far apart. It was already past two o'clock in the morning and he was on his way to the pier.

Peter slowed his stride suspiciously as he noticed a figure taking shape out of the fog and gloom in front of him. It startled him that there would be someone else walking the street at that time of morning. Cautiously he eyed the figure as it drew closer. At last he could tell it was just an old man.

Dressed in rags, head hanging low on sloping shoulders, the old man shuffled painfully toward Peter. As he neared, he stopped and, without looking, held out a shaking hand. There was a white card in the hand.

"Excuse me, sir." The man spoke in a tired voice barely above a whisper. "Can you tell me where this is?"

Suspiciously, Peter stopped and took the outstretched card. Moving closer to a street light, he could see that it was a meal ticket for a hamburger, given out by a church-funded rescue mission. But the recipient had to go to Don's Drive-In to get the food.

Without a second thought, Peter dismissed the man and sent him on this way.

"Sure, man. Just stay on this street and you'll come to it on the right."

Peter watched for a moment as the old man moved off in the direction he had indicated. Just another bum looking for a free meal, he thought to himself.

Once again on his way and thinking of the riches contained in the sock, Peter walked for several minutes and then stopped abruptly. He felt as though something had exploded in his mind.

The old man . . . alone . . . hungry . . . needing help! He was not just a bum looking for a free meal! He was a person, like Peter only a short time before, who desperately needed the caring of another human being. The man was hungry. He needed food. He needed somone for a moment to care! What if he, Peter, was supposed to be God's answer to the old man's prayer for help, just as the bikers had been his answer?

The more he thought about it, the more sure Peter became that God had just given him the opportunity to do for another human being what had been done for him! Feed him.

When he talked to the old man, Peter had known that Don's Drive-In was over five miles away and that it closed at midnight. Even if the man found it, he would not be able to get anything to eat. The least he could have done was take the old man to an all-night restaurant near the pier and buy him a hot meal. It might have cost him all of three or four dollars.

What shattered Peter most, though, was not so much the fact that he had been given the chance to be God's answer to another man's desperate prayer—it was the sad truth that he had not even recognized his chance when it stood helplessly before him! He had brushed the man off without a second thought—just as thousands had paid him no attention when he was alone and helpless.

Peter retraced his steps, hoping to find the old man. But he was gone. Forever.

Aching again with the regret he had felt so deeply, Peter once more vowed, as he had done that endless, sleepless night, never again to walk away from a hand extended in need.

It was not the ocean he saw now outside the lounge window. It was a full moon, filling the night with a beauty not its own. It was a priest, telling him to go in peace to love and serve the Lord. It was an old man, sent away hungry. It was a bird sitting on a snow-covered window ledge. Is this what the old priest meant by his story about the man and the bird on a cold winter night? Was it possible, he wondered, that the old bum on the street was sent to show Peter the way? Peter's brain burned with the fever of questions he could not answer. Overwhelmed, he gave up and forced his attention back into the room. He had a job to do and little time to do it. The bikers were expecting him at two o'clock.

As busboy, it was his job to close the lounge of the restaurant each night. That meant he cleaned all the tables, reset them for breakfast, restocked the supplies, and vacuumed the carpet. Then he was free to go.

With an effort, Peter pushed the ache in his heart out of his mind as his body began mechanically piling dirty dishes on the large tray. As he worked, his thoughts turned to the challenge that lay ahead that night.

There was going to be a raid on a rival club—the Raiders—led by the same man who had challenged Peter's right to Susan at the rock concert. A chill raced up Peter's spine at the thought of meeting the man again, this time in battle. He knew the Raiders' reputation. They were tough. And word had it they were out to replace the Saints as the controlling force in that part of the state. The challenge had to be met. There were rumors that the Raiders were already negotiating alliances with several of the smaller, less powerful clubs in the area. The result could be war between the rival factions, leaving Saints' territory vulnerable to attack by a third club.

Since diminishing membership over the past few years had left the Saints' ranks the thinnest they had been since the early days of the club, the war captains had decided an immediate and fatal blow must be dealt to the Raiders before they could establish firm footing in the area. This could be done only by an all-out raid on their headquarters near the beach.

The battle call had gone out the previous week to every available Saint, as well as to members of allied clubs still loyal to their treaty with the Saints and who also had an interest in protecting the territory from invaders. The Raiders had made no effort to hide the beach party they were hosting that night. It was hoped a surprise raid would catch them unprepared and result in a Saints' victory that would eliminate the Raider threat.

In an effort to avoid police detection, the men would travel alone or in pairs to a rendezvous a short distance from the party site.

Peter had witnessed and participated in numerous confrontations and fights during his time with the club, and he was accustomed to seeing foes back down in the face of the Saints' show of force. But Peter knew the Raiders would not back down. They would not have invaded Saints' turf if they were not prepared for the consequences.

It was one o'clock by the time Peter finished at the restaurant. The pad where he and several club members lived was empty when he got there, but he knew where the others were—at Charlie's Place just outside the city limits, a well-known and respected Saints' hangout. Changing quickly, Peter armed himself with an array of weapons and joined them.

Though the bar was loud and boisterous, few men were drinking. They had been ordered to stay sober. It was the Raiders who were supposed to get loaded.

A short time later, Peter and three others were sent out for food. They took no money with them. After a couple of minutes, the little band of marauders arrived at their destination—a small, all-night convenience store under Saints' protection. The young man behind the counter was alone. Laughing and talking loudly, the four men entered the store and collected as many sandwiches and bags of chips and cookies as they could carry. Bringing them to the checkout counter, they gathered around the clerk and watched silently as he rang up the items.

"That will be $84.25, please!" the clerk announced nervously.

Peter and the others stood silently staring at the man. The color drained from the clerk's face as he looked hopefully from one biker to the next. It was obvious the man was frightened.

"That's $84.25, please!" he tried again.

Still the bikers made no move, but remained silent, continuing to stare threateningly.

"Please, you guys! I don't want any trouble. Just pay me and leave me alone, OK?" screeched the desperate man at last, no longer able to stand quietly while they pressed close around him.

"Trouble? Did you say trouble?" Maximo asked as he suddenly leaned across the counter within an inch of the man's nose.

"No, no trouble! Please, no trouble! I don't want any trouble!" pleaded the anxious man.

"Well, m----, if you don't want trouble, why don't you give me change for the hundred dollars I gave you and we'll be on our merry way!" Maximo suggested glaringly, his voice barely above a whisper.

"You didn't give me any money!" protested the man.

"You calling me a liar, man?" Maximo asked through gritted teeth.

"No man! I guess I . . . well, I guess I just forgot!" Hurriedly he made the change and handed it to Maximo.

"And the receipt, m----!" directed the biker.

In a moment more the food was bagged and the bikers were on their way back to Charlie's Place, laughing at the fun they had just had. Peter shared their laughter.

After so many years of being beaten, abused, and intimidated by people bigger and more powerful than himself, it was exhilarating to watch someone else suffer the same fear he had known so well. How the tables had turned!

• • •

Two hours later it was all over. High on a hill overlooking a small coastal town, there is a large wooden cross. When lighted at night, it can be seen for miles in every direction. It was erected in the early 1700s by the founder of the town, a Spanish priest who moved up and down the coast establishing missions in his attempt to Christianize the existing cultures. The battle between Satan's Saints and the Raiders had taken place in the shadow of that cross.

Sitting now on the stone wall around the cross, Peter could see the lights of the town below. It was a beautiful, eerie, lonely feeling to look down on a sleeping town only hours from a new day. But it was not the silence or loneliness that bothered him this night. Many times as an adolescent, he had run away from home. With no one to turn to and nowhere to go, he would most often make his way here to this cross, standing like a guardian sentinel high above the unwary town. Here he would stay, sometimes for days, hiding in the nearby forest when necessary to avoid the occasional sightseer. Many hours had been spent sitting on this same brick wall, thinking.

Peter was sitting on the wall now, thinking. It was not the loneliness that was bothering him. Nor was it the large bruise on the side of his face or the gash that had left his arm covered with dried blood. Blood and bruises were not new to him.

It was Buck. His best friend. He was dead!

At the appointed time, about fifty Satan's Saints had rendezvoused at the rest stop along a stretch of highway only a short distance from the Raiders' party. Sheik, the son of a wealthy Arab and the undisputed leader of Satan's Saints in the south, had divided the anxious and nervous men into two groups. Riding on the hard-packed sand near the breaking surf, one group would attack from the south and the other from the north. Sheik was sure this pincher tactic, along with the element of total surprise and the strung-out condition the Raiders would surely be in after partying most of the night would result in so much confusion that it would be a sure rout for the Saints.

It had all sounded so good. What had happened? Peter and Buck had ridden in with the group coming from the south. Although it was hard to tell in the darkness around the campfire, it appeared to Peter there were only about half as many Raiders as there were Saints. It looked as if it were going to be easy. But just as the north and south groups converged on the Raiders and the battle began, another large group of Raiders armed with knives, chains, and crowbars came pouring out of the rocks that lined the shore and pinned the Saints against the water's edge. It had been a trap! The Raiders had staged the party only to draw the Saints out into the open.

Peter shuddered as he recalled the fierce hand-to-hand fighting. Fortunately, it had lasted only a few minutes. At the sound of sirens, all the men had rushed for their bikes in an attempt to escape the clutches of the riot squad. Someone had tipped the police and they arrived just in time. But not in time to save Buck. Somewhere, somehow, in the mass of struggling bodies, Buck had been hit in the face with an object that killed him. During the wild dash to get away, Peter had seen him lying in the sand, his face crushed and unrecognizable, his head half buried in the blood-stained sand.

Like most of the others, Peter escaped the police by racing down the beach. But the shock of Buck's death sent him wandering aimlessly around dark and deserted back roads until at last he found himself sitting alone on the wall at the foot of the cross.

Although he himself had been beaten almost to death at the hands of his adopted parents, the reality of Buck's death left Peter stunned. Everything had happened so quickly and unexpectedly. One moment they were laughing and talking. The next, Peter could hardly recognize him, except for the clothes he was wearing. It was all so sudden and so terribly final.

For hours, Peter grieved over the loss of a comrade and struggled to overcome his shock of coming face to face with the fragility of life.

He soon realized a part of himself had died with Buck that night. With the passing of his friend, the truth began to crystalize in his feverish and troubled mind. As the image of Buck's crushed face flashed again and again before his mind's eye, it slowly began to take on the shape and form of another face. His own! The more he looked at Buck lying dead on the beach, the more Peter saw himself.

If he continued to live within the club in the life-style he had chosen, sooner or later it would be his body lying with a crushed face on the sand of some lonely beach. His turn would come! It was inevitable. If he were not killed outright in a fight, he would surely be killed in another even more tragic way. Sooner or later the law would capture him with enough evidence to result in a conviction. If that should happen, he would probably spend the rest of his life in prison, locked up like an animal in a living coffin with other living dead. Given a choice, he would rather die than sit and rot in a cell.

Peter knew as surely as he was sitting on that wall that if something in his life did not change drastically, and soon, death or prison would be his fate. He wanted neither. He had already been forced to endure one tour of hell as a child; he certainly did not want to sentence himself to another.

The crisp cool breeze, the sharp, clear night spotted by bright pinpricks of city lights seemed to clear Peter's thinking of the confusion that had so possessed it for the past several years. From the perspective of the cross, the world stretched out below him, and his place in it began to make sense. Maybe he was not an alien misfit in a world of people who knew where they belonged. Maybe there could be a place there for him too.

The remaining hours before sunrise were spent thinking about where he had been, where he was going, where he wanted to go, and how to get there. At times his thoughts filled him with self-pity. But just as suddenly they would turn to anger and rage. He would pick up a rock and hurl it viciously at the city and its sleeping inhabitants far below. But mostly, he just thought and wondered.

What was the meaning of it all? Why had it happened? And why to him? Was he really so bad as to deserve the beatings? What had he done to make people want to hurt him, when he so desperately wanted them to care for him? There was no doubt something was wrong with him. But what? If he only knew, maybe he could do something to change it. He was programmed to survive. But how?

Like a rat trying to find its way out of a maze, Peter's mind raced through his days, blindly seeking the way to freedom from his history, his nightmares, his memories—but especially, from his fear.

He could see lights begin to go on in some of the houses scattered about the town as the heavy darkness began to fade with the coming dawn. Lighting another cigarette, he shifted his weight on the wall and leisurely prepared to allow the morning to come to meet him.

That morning it became clear to Peter—if he were ever to find the way he sought, if he were ever to achieve peace and freedom, if he were ever to know the assurance of another's trust and love, he must seek these things himself. He was sure no one would bring them to him. He would have to take control of his own life and point it in the direction that most promised fulfillment.

As the possibilities of change blossomed within his mind, Peter began to sense a growing excitement, an expectancy. It flooded over him like an ocean swell as the eastern skyline exploded in rapturous colors, making its cosmic announcement one more time.

As the first arc of big bright sun showed over the distant horizon, Peter knew what he must do. Although he did not know how he was going to do it, he knew he must give life one honest shot. Somehow, somewhere, he must make an all-out effort to reclaim his life from the fate for which it appeared destined, though he probably would not succeed. But the instinct to survive was so strong, he knew he must at least try.

But how? How does one go about turning a life around? How does one take something dirty and bad, and make it into something clean and good? That question would perplex and torment Peter for the next several years.

Peter had no way of knowing then, sitting alone on that wall at the foot of the cross, watching one of the most glorious sunrises he had ever seen, that he had already begun. He had made a choice. He knew the way he lived now would lead to death. Instead, he had chosen life!

He also did not know it was Easter morning.

PART TWO

REDEEMING THE DAMNED

Introduction

With his commitment to the bikers and their way of life shaken, and deeply disturbed by Buck's death, Peter became preoccupied with thoughts of changing his life. Overwhelmed by the meaninglessness of the death of his friend and the senselessness of a life doomed to self-destruction, he began his relentless search for answers. How does a man go about changing his life? How do you take what is and make it into what might be, or what could be?

Buck would have told him that power is the answer. You must have power over others if you are to improve your life. There is protection and security in power. Only the strong survive.

The old priest would tell him something entirely different. Jesus is the answer, he would say. Only he is the Way. If Peter were to save his life, he must lose it—surrender it to God in faith and pursue a life of service to others. The meek shall inherit the earth.

Then there were others who would assure him that money is the answer. He must seek a better job and more money. Money can buy the changes he desires. It is the rich who control the world. Money talks. It can also move mountains.

Just as important, what should he change? His friends? Residence? Job? Clothes?

Dizzy with confusion and uncertainty, Peter stumbled blindly through the next several weeks in a whirlwind of questions with no answers. Everywhere he turned seemed to lead to a dead end; every avenue was blocked by an impenetrable barrier. He could not pursue power because of his personal weakness and inadequacy. He could not pursue money because of his ignorance and unmarketability. He could not pursue a discipleship of Christ because of his incredible unworthiness. He was bad. Some people even thought him evil. There was no place for him among the faithful. And yet, the priest had told him God loved him so much that he had sent his Son to show him the way. How could this be? Even more important, why would God bother? Everyone else had written him off as a lost cause.

A part of Peter believed what he had heard from the people who had helped shape his personal identity and beliefs. Still another part of him believed the priest. Who was telling the truth? Both could not be right.

Then it came to him like a fog lifting suddenly from his mind. He was walking along the beach late one night, thinking about his dilemma, depressed and confused as usual, when the answer came. It was not his friends he had to change, or his residence, his job, or his clothes. What he had to change was his mind! The barrier that stood between him and change was his thinking. Believing himself to be bad allowed no possibility that he was not. He had to change his thinking from illusion to truth. He must pursue truth in all things, in all people, at all times. *Truth* is the answer!

With this thought also came the realization of what he must do. He must train and educate his mind to seek truth. He must go back to school. It was the *truth* that would set him free from the prison of his past. It was *truth* that would make possible the necessary changes in his life.

Suddenly motivated, Peter applied for admission to college. He was excited. And frightened. But if there were an answer, he was determind to find it!

Six

Being accepted into the community junior college was the easy part. The application procedure was simple and brief. Peter's high school grades were adequate—not high enough to attract attention or low enough to cause concern. On paper he looked like most other young people from the local high schools who decided to spend a year or two in junior college before transferring to a major state school. Although he would have to rearrange his work schedule at the restaurant, by June of that year Peter knew he was going back to school.

The hard part would be staying in school—submitting to the authority of a teacher, trying to live up to others' expectations, conforming. The achievement of academic standards was not as disturbing to Peter as the challenge of having to interact with other people. He could control his grades; he could not control other people. Relationships frightened him.

Filled with anxiety and self-doubt, he left his bike in the parking lot and strutted arrogantly onto the campus, notebook in hand, for his first class. Dressed in his usual denims and boots, with no shirt under his colors vest, he made his way slowly to the Language Arts building at the heart of the campus. Here he would take English 1A. The red bandana he was using as a head band to keep his long hair out of his face felt tight across his forehead.

Peter pretended not to notice the stares as he passed, or the hushed conversations as he drew near, or the moving out of his way. But seeing people react to his presence as he was used to having them behave made him feel more confident. They might not like him and they might not accept him, but they knew he was there! That was enough for now.

Avoiding the eyes of the cluster of young people near the door, Peter entered the classroom and took a seat exactly in the middle of the room. There were as many seats to the right as to the left, to the front as behind.

Leaning back, Peter lit a cigarette, stretched his long legs out in the aisle, and tried to appear relaxed as other students began filing into the room and claiming seats. A growing nervousness began to take hold of him as he heard people sitting down behind him. It made him uncomfortable to have people behind him. His instinct was to move to a corner of the room where he could sit with his back to a wall and see the entire room. But to move now would make him appear unsure of himself, even vulnerable. He could not take that risk. Appearances were too important.

Seeing no ashtrays, Peter dropped the cigarette butt on the floor and smashed it out with his boot as the teacher entered the room. She was young and attractive—not what Peter had expected! Suddenly self-conscious and feeling terribly out of place, he now regretted his appearance. It made him stand out. Even more, he regretted all the empty seats two deep around him. Though the class was full, no one wanted to claim a seat so close to him.

After introducing herself as Mrs. Williams and welcoming them all to the class, the teacher turned her eyes directly upon Peter. They brought a warmth to him that caught him by surprise—until she spoke.

"And for those of you who have not learned to read, you will notice the sign directly behind me which says No Smoking. An individual's right to smoke," she continued, now scanning the rest of the class, "does not deprive the rest of us of our right to breathe clean air!" Again she returned her eyes to Peter.

The warmth Peter had felt now turned ice cold. With his jaw shut tight, he hooded his eyes in emptiness and stared unresponsively at the woman as his mind raced to fully comprehend the situation. It was obvious she was talking directly to him. He already felt like a freak, and her criticism only made the feeling deepen. What the hell was he doing here anyway? Some pipe dream about getting an education. Making something of himself! Well hell, he was something already. He was a Saint! Now that was something!

Embarrassed, Peter decided to take the offensive. He stood slowly, walked to the front of the room, and sat on the edge of the teacher's desk. She watched him cautiously. Taking out a cigarette, he lit it, took a deep drag, and blew the smoke in her direction. Then with a smile, he offered her one from his pack.

"Wanna smoke?"

"No thanks," she eyed him critically. "Smoking is forbidden in the classrooms."

"Is that so?" Peter smiled at her.

"Would you be kind enough to smoke in the hallway, please?"

"Only if you will join me," he answered, his eyes fixed upon her like a cat on a mouse.

"Not only are you violating a rule," she warned him seriously, "but you are also disturbing the class. These people are here to learn, not to play games. Now you either put out that cigarette and sit down, or I will have to report this incident to administration."

"You're cute," Peter answered her warning without moving his eyes from hers. He saw self-consciousness stir in their depths. For a moment they clung fiercely to his, then dropped away to sweep the floor. A flush appeared in her cheeks. Embarrassment? Or anger?

Peter could hear the nervous shifting of weight in desks all over the room. The air was filled with electric expectancy at the unexpected confrontation. She had made him look foolish in front of the class. He had to get even, to show them all that no woman, even if she was the teacher, was going to make a fool of him and get away with it.

"Now look," she spoke again after regaining her composure. Her voice was softer now, more feminine, and contained just a hint of pleading. "I don't know who you are or what you want. But I don't want any trouble. All I want to do is conduct this class as I am paid to do. But in order for me to do my job, you have to do yours. And part of your job is to obey the rules."

Peter watched her for a long moment more, puffing silently. At last sure of his victory, he stepped on the butt and stood up.

"No problem," he said, and returned to his seat.

The class was to meet from seven to ten in the evening, Monday, Wednesday, and Friday for six weeks. A fifteen-minute break was taken midway in each class. This night was no exception.

Peter stepped out of the building during the break to smoke and get away from the curious, resentful, and defensive stares of his classmates. Neither did he want another run-in with Mrs. Williams.

He was surprised when she appeared before him out of the dark, accompanied by a man. After introducing himself as the assistant dean of student affairs, the man proceeded to inform Peter of the school's policy on smoking in the classroom, pointing out that the rule originated with the state fire marshall's office and was intended for the benefit of all, not just a few.

"We have to do things a certain way around here whether we like it or not," he concluded, looking hard at Peter, unmoved from the brick wall upon which he sat. "Those people who do not like it can do one of two things: They can either buckle under or get out. You get my drift?"

"Yeah, man, I hear you," Peter answered sullenly.

"If you're here because you want an education, fine! You'll get it. But if you're here to look for trouble, you won't have to look far, because it will find you!"

Peter watched silently as the man turned abruptly on his heel and disappeared with Mrs. Williams in the gloom. For a moment he had to fight the urge to put a knot at the base of the man's skull. Seething with rage, he smoked another cigarette to help himself calm down. He knew flying off the handle would only bring him trouble. The man was right. He did not want trouble. He wanted an education. In order to get what he wanted, he would have to play by the rules—their rules. There was no other way.

Still upset and frustrated, Peter decided not to return to the class. He did not want to see Mrs. Williams again. Instead, he took a walk around the campus. As he neared the student center and snack bar aglow with lights and milling people, his attention was drawn to a man sitting alone at one of the tables. He was concentrating on a board game in front of him. Peter recognized it as chess. But what caught his attention was the man's hair and beard. They were even longer than his own. He stood out in the crowd. Peter could relate to that.

"What's happenin', man?" He approached the man cautiously, not knowing what to expect.

"What's happenin', brother?" the man answered, looking up.

Peter was surprised. The man was old! He must be at least forty! An old hippie!

"You playin' by yourself?" Peter asked, indicating the chess set with a nod.

"No one else seems to know how to play," the man nodded with a light laugh. "Guess it's a lost art! You play?" He eyed Peter curiously.

"Never learned. But I want to. Don't suppose you would teach me?" There were few things about himself that Peter admired. But his mind was one of them. He could think! In a world that reminded him so often of his inadequacies, it was his only source of pride. "You'd have some competition then!"

"That's cool!" the man responded without a second thought. "Sit down. Ed's my name. What yours?"

Thus began a friendship that would result not only in learning to play chess—in itself a significant achievement—but would prove vitally important in the early days and months of Peter's attempt to change his life course. He recognized the irony of their meeting as he recalled it much later in life. Had he not had the confrontation with the English teacher and the dean, he probably would have returned to the classroom on that first night. Had he done that, he most likely would not have met Ed.

Although Peter could not know it at their first meeting, Ed was important to him because he had already traveled the way Peter was going. A refugee from his own past life, the man was a cultural bridge between Peter's past and future. He had made the transition from outlaw to renegade and now became a guide, a model, for Peter. That transition was going to be the greatest challenge of Peter's young life. He would need all the help he could get. Much of that help came from Ed.

Peter had registered to take three courses during his first semester of college. In addition to the English course, he attempted introductory courses in psychology and philosophy. He was particularly interested in the philosophy class. He was already intimately acquainted with the struggle to comprehend the nature of humanity, truth, goodness, and reality, though in less formal settings.

Peter's first semester in college lasted almost two weeks. During those two weeks he attended class religiously, doing the assignments as best he could. His grades reflected his ability, but not his full potential. He particularly liked meeting Ed after class to talk and play a game of chess before calling it a night.

As hard as he tried during those early days, Peter could not seem to fit in with the other students and the routine. He had repeated confrontations with Mrs. Williams and one of the other teachers. It was not that he wanted trouble; it was as though he was as sensitive to pushing and pressure as an extremely sore thumb might be. So aware of his inadequacies and differences, the looks, words, and expectations of others became like blows against which he had to defend himself. Everything and everybody was a threat. He felt the straight world would destroy him unless he protected himself by fighting back. Hiding behind his colors and image, as well as his appearance, was not enough.

The inevitable happened one night while the class was on break. Peter had stretched out on a bench near Ed, with his hands pillowing his head. Closing his eyes, he had allowed his mind to drift off into the sexual fantasy that had teased his mind from that first day in class—a physical relationship with Mrs. Williams. The emotional satisfaction he experienced was as meaningful to him as the physical pleasure derived in the fantasy.

Suddenly his mind exploded in a flash of red, orange, and yellow as the pain on his stomach reached his brain at the same time as the sound of a slap reached his ears.

As he lay on the bench, his vest had fallen open, exposing his bare stomach. Someone had just slapped him with an open hand. Without thinking, Peter went berserk.

It was only with Ed shouting in his ear and pulling at him that Peter began to regain his senses. As the violence of his sudden rage began to diminish, he became aware that he was on his knees with his arms wrapped tightly around the neck of a man held firmly against his chest. The man's face was ash white, despite the blood pouring from his nose and several deep scratches.

"You're gonna kill him, man!" screamed Ed in his ear as he tried desperately to break Peter's hold. "Turn him loose, man, turn him loose!"

Slowly color returned to the man's face as Peter released his grip. He recognized the man as a student who had tried to strike up a conversation with him on several occasions. Frightened by the attempted friendship, Peter had used the man's short hair and clean-shaven face as an excuse to avoid him. Now he was trying to kill him! Why?

"What the h---'s wrong with you!" shouted the frightened man as he struggled to his feet. "You d----- near killed me! H---, man, I didn't mean anything by slapping you."

So that was it, Peter thought to himself. He had been slapped on the stomach. That explained it.

"I'm sorry, man," he tried to apologize, his voice barely above a whisper. "I didn't mean to hurt you. It's just that . . . "

"Didn't mean to hurt me? What the h--- do you call this?" the now angry man shouted back, indicating his bloody face.

"Look, man. I'm sorry. But you slapped me on the stomach . . . " Peter tried to explain again. But the man was in no mood to listen.

"Get the h--- away from me! I didn't hurt you. All I did was slap you. And you go crazy!" The man began backing away. "You're crazy, man. Something's wrong with you!" And the man disappeared in the darkness.

Devastated, Peter stared for a long time at the spot where the man had vanished. A part of him wanted to run after him, to apologize, to make him understand. Another part kept him frozen in his tracks. Why bother? The man wouldn't understand. How could he? Maybe something *was* seriously wrong with him. Maybe the man was right. But crazy?

Peter sensed Ed's presence at his elbow before he felt his hand on his shoulder.

"What happened to you, man?" he asked softly.

"I don't know. It's crazy!"

"I've seen that kind of violence before. When I was riding with the Bad Guys. One of the guys in the club would go crazy if you hit him on certain parts of his body. I mean he would go c-r-a-z-y! I think it's called a homicidal rage."

"Yeah, I guess I'm like that," Peter mused. "I was beaten so much on the stomach when I was a kid, I can't stand to have anyone hit me there. I can't explain it!"

Depression filled the void left by the rage. Overwhelmed by his own lack of control, Peter went back to the pad that night and locked himself in the bedroom. For two days he did not move except to use the bathroom. Neither did he sleep. Despite the efforts of the other Saints living in the apartment, Peter remained silent and unmoved, withdrawn totally inside himself as though the world were not the only threat to his life. Perhaps he himself was the greatest threat.

He missed his classes. It was just as well, though. The letter came on the second day. It was from the dean of student affairs. He had been expelled.

Seven

His name was Michael—an attorney in town. Peter met him at the restaurant. He came in every day around noon, sat at the bar in the lounge near Peter's station, and had a couple of drinks. He seemed lonely. There was never anyone with him and he did not seem to know anyone else in the lounge. Day after day Peter watched him enter, have his drinks, then leave an hour or so later without having talked with a soul. He felt sorry for the man and eventually struck up a conversation with him. He seemed friendly and eager to talk. And intelligent. Peter had few opportunities to be involved in intellectual discussions, and never with a practicing attorney who not only held his attention but had his respect.

In his attempt to change his life, Peter had decided that one of the things he must do was associate with people who embodied the character and qualities he wanted for himself. So he was looking for new friends. Maybe this was an opportunity. The fact that the man was an attorney also intrigued Peter. He had experience with attorneys, but never as friends.

For this reason Peter agreed when, a few days before the letter from the dean arrived, Michael asked him if he would like to have dinner with him. He had no family, he told Peter, and hated to eat alone.

For Peter, friendship was a political, social, or economic alliance between two persons for their mutual benefit. Having a friend meant you were no longer alone in your attempt to survive, to make your way in a hostile and dangerous place. The difference between himself and people like Michael was that they were less vulnerable, and so less threatened. From Peter's perspective, education and wealth were the means by which to overcome dependencies, the source of all vulnerabilities. In his mind, to *need* no one was to remain safe from everyone.

Unfortunately, at this stage in his life Peter was well aware that in order to acquire the wealth and education that would set him free, he would first have to work at a job and attend a school. Both his employer and his instructors became masters in his world—masters to be resented, resisted, and yet respected. They had what he wanted and could get nowhere else—a paycheck and a grade. Peter became painfully aware of just how much his destiny rested with such people. Failure to please them might result in their turning against him as his parents had done. A failing grade or a final paycheck could alter the course of his life. He resented other people having such control of his life! Unable to please his parents, Peter was sure he would fail in his attempts to meet the minimum standards of performance set for him on the job and in school. And yet, he had to try! He had no choice. His only hope was to push ahead, on the one hand slaving to meet their expectations, and on the other, fighting desperately to keep himself from self-destructing in a moment of despair and panic.

It was here that friends could be most helpful. A friend could help ease the panic, slow the retreat, make sense of the chaos, and, even more important, stop the flow of essential life forces from self-inflicted wounds intended not so much to maim as to destroy. A friend could be a comrade in arms in the battle to survive.

The possibility of a friendship along with the assurance of a free steak dinner were all Peter needed to accept Michael's invitation. After picking him up, Michael drove several miles out of town to a large well-known restaurant. They were seated immediately, though there were people waiting in line. That impressed Peter. From the waiter's attitude, Michael was either a popular regular or someone pretty special.

Michael ordered Beefeaters on the rocks for both of them, with instructions to the waiter to continue replacing empty glasses with full ones until told to stop.

This was great! Not only was he getting a free meal, he was going to get all the booze he could drink. Lighting a cigarette, Peter settled himself comfortably for what he perceived was going to be a good evening.

Although he had built up a tolerance for alcohol while living with the bikers, some of whom always seemed to have a beer in hand, Peter began to feel the effects of the alcohol by the fifth drink. His head and body began to feel lighter, and many of the things Michael was saying seemed more humorous than at first. It felt good to relax and laugh.

After the waiter had brought their sixth Beefeater, the conversation took a twist. It was such a subtle change Peter did not notice it at first.

"I really like you a lot!" Michael said matter-of-factly while peering intently at Peter over his upraised glass. "A lot!"

It was the second "a lot" that caught Peter's attention. It was not so much that it was said as *how* it was said. There was an element of expectancy in the statement that was initially disturbing.

"Yes, I am thinking of going on a world cruise—buying a large yacht, hiring a small crew, and setting sail for parts unknown," Michael continued. "You like to travel, Peter?"

"Really haven't done a lot of it," Peter answered, trying hard to keep his words from slurring together. "Never had the money."

"What would you say if I invited you to join me on the cruise? All expenses paid?"

"Are you serious?" Peter asked incredulously.

"Yeah, I am. I'll even buy you a new wardrobe for the occasion. You will want for nothing. I mean nothing," Michael reiterated smoothly as he reached across the table and placed his hand on Peter's arm. "I'll take care of everything."

Suddenly uncomfortable, Peter moved his arm and sat back in his chair, forcing his mind and eyes to clear. Years of survival living had taught him incredible control of his senses. It also had taught him that nothing is free; everything comes with a price tag.

"Sounds exciting. And expensive," he mumbled.

"Money's no problem. H--- man, I'm rich! Some people tell me I've got more money than good sense. Anyway, I'm loaded. Always have been. My parents were rich and passed it on to me. No, Peter, I have known all the pleasures this life has to offer," Michael mused as though confiding a long-kept secret. "All but one, that is. And unfortunately that one is by far the most important!"

"Yeah? What's that, man?"

"A special relationship with someone I really care about and who cares about me. You know what I mean? That something special that comes along once in a lifetime. I need to love someone, Peter. Someone like you."

Suddenly it all came clear. Michael was gay! This whole thing—the dinner, the cruise, the promises, everything—was not an offering of friendship, but of perverted sex.

Peter's initial reaction was one of rage. He wanted to unleash his fury at the man by beating his face to a pulp. Not only was he offended that the man would think he also might be gay, but he reacted violently to the thought of being used, manipulated, exploited by another human being. But nothing of his reaction reached his face.

After the initial shock wore off, Peter began to consider how best to handle the situation. Although he continued to resent the implication, he remembered the possible value a friendship with an attorney might have in the future. He decided to attempt to salvage what he could from the relationship. At a deeper, more personal level, he was touched by the desperation he could sense in the man's attempt to lure him into intimacy. He related to it out of his own childhood experience of needing someone—anyone—to love him.

Knowing that physically the man was no threat, and secure in his own sexual identity, Peter decided not to be defensive toward this man and his obvious problem, but rather to try to help him. What a profound shift in perspective! Always before he had viewed his relationships with all persons from a self-protective viewpoint, believing failure to do so would result in pain, suffering, and rejection. For the first time in his life, Peter believed another human being had a problem more threatening than his own. And he wanted to help. The question was, How? How does a nobody go about helping a somebody? What did he possibly have to offer this man that could help him?

"I know what you mean, man," Peter empathized as a seed began to take hold in his thoughts. "I guess I've never really had anyone to love me either. Sometimes I get to wondering if I will ever find a woman who could love me. I mean really love me, you know what I mean?"

"Yes, I think so," Michael murmured and continued to watch Peter closely.

"I guess my mother loved me. But I don't know that. You see," Peter continued, "I didn't grow up with my parents. I had to grow up in foster homes, and later an adopted home."

Peter talked endlessly through the next half hour and another drink. Michael listened without interrupting. Peter told him of Bo, the dog he had loved so much on the farm before he was adopted. He told of their special and loving relationship—that Bo would never hurt him and always wanted to be near him. He told him about sunrises—that no matter what happened each day, he could always count on the sun rising the next day. He talked about his brothers—that he loved them so much he would do anything for them. He talked about love and what it meant to him.

"I used to think love was a feeling," Peter continued calmly, his head resting on his fist as he talked to Michael. "You know, man, something you felt for another person. But if love is a feeling, then love can change, because feelings change. You can't count on them to stay the same. How do you build a life or a relationship on something you can't trust to be the same tomorrow as today? No, man! Not me! If love is a feeling, then I want none of it!"

"Wait a minute," Michael interjected curiously. "If love is not a feeling, then what is it?"

"It's a relationship, man! A relationship. Loving someone is treating them so they become a better person because of it. It is the same today, tomorrow, and yesterday. It remains the same. You can count on it, trust it when all else fails. H---, man, I don't want someone to *feel* good about me! What I need is someone to *treat me like a human being!*"

"I'd never thought about it like that." Michael seemed to be pondering the idea. A long silence hung between the two as they explored their own thoughts. At last Michael spoke again. "How do you know this love exists? Have you found someone to love you this way?"

"Yeah, man, I have!" Peter exclaimed, suddenly excited. "There is someone who loves me like that!"

"But I thought you said you had not found that 'someone special' in your life."

"No, man, I haven't found a wife. I'm talking about something else. Listen!" Peter exclaimed urgently as he inched closer to the table, leaning toward the man on the other side. "Maybe you'll understand better if I tell you a story. It goes like this . . . There was an old man sitting in his study, reading, late one wintry night. It was cold and dark outside. He had a fire blazing in the fireplace. It was warm and cozy in the room. Suddenly he heard a pecking at the window . . . "

The words of the old priest seemed to flow easily. Michael listened intently, totally absorbed in what Peter was saying.

"Don't you see, man? God is love. And he loves us so much he would actually send his Son to become one of us so he could show us the way. He loves us! You and me. He doesn't talk about it or feel it. He does it! We don't have to go through the rest of our lives feeling alone. Or unwanted. Or bad. There is someone who really does care!"

Peter could hardly believe it was his voice saying these things. It was as though it was not really him talking, but someone else—someone who was using his mind and his voice to reach the man. Where are these words coming from? he wondered. Do I really believe what I hear myself saying, or are they just words? Somewhere in the back of his mind, he again heard his mother's voice, singing the words he was only now beginning to understand. "Jesus loves me, this I know . . . "

Michael seemed to melt in the warmth of Peter's sincerity. Tears came to his eyes, and at last he settled his head on his oustretched arms and wept. Peter just let him cry. How many times had he, too, wept similar tears?

They continued to talk for another hour or so, paying little attention to the people around them. It was as though they were in a world of their own, or their discussion was so important nothing else mattered. Michael said no more about a cruise.

Peter felt good when they left the restaurant. The two shook hands as he got out of the car at his pad. Michael thanked him for the company, promised to drop in at the restaurant in the next couple of days, and was gone.

Still light-headed from the drinks he had consumed, Peter took a walk around the block before sacking out. He expected to sleep well that night because of the alcohol. But he did not. His sleep was restless, filled with dreams and feelings he had not experienced for a long time.

At first the dream was vague and obscure. The woman and girl, whom he knew to be his mother and sister, did not have faces. He *felt* their presence more than he knew them by sight. But in the dream they were a long way off. And something separated them from him—something he could not cross or get past. It was not a wall, or a valley, or anything physical, but an emptiness—a void that should never have existed, that existed only because the people it separated existed. What separated the dreamer from the forms in his dream was a period of time—a vast chasm of fourteen years without shared space, or shared memories, or shared joys or sorrows, or pain, or loving. How do you bridge fourteen years of difference? Or nothingness?

As the dream progressed, Peter began to panic. The harder he struggled to reach the shadowy figures, the farther they seemed to withdraw and the greater the emptiness between them. And yet he had to reach them! Desperately, he tried to find a way. Slowly the figures grew smaller and smaller and Peter was a small boy in the back seat of a car, watching his mother through the rear window until at last she was out of sight.

"No, no, no!" he heard himself scream as he sat bolt upright in the darkness, his heart pounding madly, his body tense and twitching. The clothes he still wore from the night before were drenched in sweat. After a few moments the panic subsided and he became aware of where he was. He had had a nightmare. The overwhelming urge to beg, scream, curse, and cry all at the same time diminished as he became more and more aware of the nature of his dream.

It had been several years since he had consciously thought about his lost family. Once in the adopted family, all his energy and concentration had been focused on surviving. Slowly as time moved on, one year after another, the images of his parents and brother and sister grew more and more vague until at last he could not really remember what they looked like. Only the feelings remained. As the images grew dimmer, the feelings grew stronger and deeper until at last they were what he wanted and needed them to be.

Now, after all those years, they had come back. Try as he might to dismiss them in the days that followed, he could not. They remained with him like an unfinished task. He knew that sooner or later he must try to find his family. Somehow. Somewhere. The chances were good they all were still out there somewhere, living their lives like other people. Peter was sure the dreams would continue until he did find them.

He tried to go back to sleep in the early hours of the morning but could not. A restlessness that possessed both his mind and body sent him walking while his mind sought to order his thoughts, his heart struggled against old feelings.

Was it a coincidence that he found himself at the church? He could have walked to a thousand different places. Why that church where the old priest had told him the story of the bird? Peter was as curious and amazed then as he is to this day.

For whatever reason, Peter was sitting alone early that Wednesday morning in the back pew of the empty church. The lights around the altar were dim, filling the church with a gentle softness Peter found comforting. Lost in his own troubled thoughts, he was surprised when the sacristy door opened and the old priest stepped into the sanctuary.

At first Peter was offended by his presence, as though he had selfishly invaded Peter's special time, totally uninvited. But something about that wise old face made Peter relax. Perhaps it was the hint of a smile that crossed it when the priest saw Peter sitting alone in the empty church. Or maybe it was the fact that he did not seem surprised to find him there, as though he had always been there, a natural part of what was taking place. Or even more important, maybe it was because the priest just left him alone, without expectation. Whatever it was, Peter felt comfortable enough to remain for the service that included only the two of them.

"You seem changed since we last met," observed the priest when the service was over and he had walked to the rear of the church.

"Yeah, how?"

"You don't seem as angry."

"Well, maybe. But it's temporary."

"All change is. What is important is where it leads us," the priest said, looking kindly at him. "Do you know where it is leading you?"

Suddenly Peter was a little uncomfortable. He certainly knew where he was coming from. But had no clear idea where he was going. Being asked about it confused him, made him feel inadequate. He wanted to avoid the question. But instead, he answered.

"No."

"Well, few of us do." The priest placed his arm around Peter's shoulders as they moved outside. "That is why few of us ever get where we're going. Does that make sense?"

"I'm not sure," Peter answered, not wanting to disclose that he did not have a clue as to what the man was talking about.

"You see, young man," the priest elaborated, "if you do not know where you are going, then any road will do. Right? And if just any old road will do, then you are likely to end up just anywhere instead of the somewhere you may want to go. Understand?"

"I see what you mean. I guess it helps to know where you're going, huh?"

"Undoubtedly! But the problem is that most of the rest of us have no more idea where we are going than you do!"

"Don't you?" Peter asked, surprised that he would have anything in common with the priest.

"No, no more than the next man, I guess, although at times I would like to think so! And I certainly want other people to think so. That is part of my job."

"You mean you are like me?" Peter asked incredulously, the thought both intriguing and disturbing. If the priest did not have a clear idea of where he was going and what life was all about, who did?

"Not exactly, son. We are alike in that neither of us knows exactly where we are headed in life. We share that commonality. But I am different in a very important way. You see, Peter," he spoke the name as though ringing a bell in reverent respect, "although I do not have a clear understanding of just where my life is taking me, I *do* know the way to get there!"

"You know what?" Again Peter was confused.

"I know the way to get where I am going!" the priest stated again, a twinkle in his eye as he watched Peter struggle with the thought.

"And what way is that?" Peter asked after a moment.

Stopping to look Peter square in the eye, the old priest smiled warmly.

"Jesus is the way," he said at last. A long pause hung between them as Peter thought this over. It frightened him in a way. A part of him wanted to bolt, while another part wanted to hear more.

"Moreover," the priest continued, "I know no other way is possible!"

"Can Jesus show me where to find my mother?" Peter blurted as anger began to surge within him. He was embarrassed the moment the words left his lips.

The priest looked at him curiously, concern showing in his eyes.

"Why don't you join me for breakfast?" he said. "You can tell me more about your mother."

"Naw, forget it, man! I've got to split!" Suddenly Peter had to leave. He had not meant to say what he did. It made him feel exposed, vulnerable. Leaving quickly, he was soon out of sight.

His conversation with the priest echoed in his mind as he made his way home. He could think of nothing else.

Passing a restaurant along the way, Peter decided to stop for a cup of coffee and collect his thoughts. There was a morning edition of the paper lying on an unoccupied table by the window. His mind full of torment, Peter sat down and absentmindedly flipped it open to the front page. There in bold headlines across the top of the front page was an announcement: Well-Known Local Attorney Dies in Fiery Crash. Michael was dead. Peter had been the last person to see him alive.

Eight

Crushed by Michael's death and feeling a total failure after being expelled from school, Peter's depression could have lasted a lifetime. It lasted two days instead. The third day was Saturday. But not just any Saturday. It was graduation Saturday—the day Jimmy, his next younger brother was scheduled to graduate from advanced infantry training at the Marine Corps base. It had been four months since Peter had seen him off at the bus station on his way to boot camp. Knowing that no one else would be there to celebrate Jimmy's graduation, and to pick him up for his two-week liberty, Peter had promised that nothing would keep him away.

He felt his spirits lift with the exhilaration that came with riding his bike carelessly through big-city traffic on his way to the camp. It made him feel free and uninhibited. His excitement mounted as freeway signs announced the fast-approaching exit.

Peter eased his way into the line of traffic moving slowly past the guard station at the entrance of the base. Refusing to look, he could feel the car behind him pressed only inches from his rear tire. The revving engine told him the driver would like nothing better than to relieve the world of yet more vermin.

He could not help smiling as the corporal at the gate issued him a visitor's pass, spitting out the mandatory "Thank you, sir!" through gritted teeth. It was obvious the soldier resented not only Peter's dress and mode of transportation, but especially his freedom.

Like the other guests, Peter watched the graduation exercises from the bleachers erected for that purpose. Try as he might, he could not find his brother among the several hundred graduating recruits. They all looked strangely alike.

At the conclusion of the ceremonies, the recruits returned to their barracks for liberty check-out while their waiting families and friends found refreshments in the welcome center. Fearful of crowds, Peter returned to his bike in the parking lot and waited for his brother there.

A half-hour passed. Peter watched the happy reunion of recruits with their families. But his brother was not among them. Still he waited. Another half-hour. Soon all the other guests were gone.

Peter was confused and a little worried. He was sure this

was the right day. And his brother had said to wait for him in the visitor's parking lot. So where was he? Peter decided not to wait any longer.

Entering the welcome center, he saw a sergeant in full-dress blues sitting at a table littered with papers. Peter waited until he had the sergeant's attention. He watched the soldier's eyes change from open curiosity to flashing resentment, then to that empty look that hides true feelings when acting by force of military courtesy rather than by choice. He explained the situation.

"Wait here, *sir!* I'll get the lieutenant," the sergeant barked without emotion and exited through a rear door.

Peter had time to smoke three cigarettes before the sergeant returned with a lieutenant. The sergeant sat down at his desk. The lieutenant moved crisply toward Peter.

"You the private's brother?" he asked as he neared.

"That's right. I'm here to take him home on his liberty. Where is he?" Peter met the lieutenant's gaze.

"The private's liberty has been cancelled."

"Cancelled? Why was it cancelled? Everybody else got liberty, didn't they? Why can't he have his liberty?" Peter demanded, feeling righteous anger begin to burn within him.

"He's reassigned to Papa Company for convalescence."

"What the h--- do you mean, convalescence?" Peter was now all ears and burning to know what was going on.

"He had an accident about an hour ago." The lieutenant spoke reluctantly. It was obvious to Peter that he did not want to give him any more information than he had to.

"Accident?" Peter shouted. "What accident? What the h--- is going on here? Talk to me, d--- it, or I'll tear this place apart!"

"Calm down, mister!" the lieutenant spoke firmly, but dropped his military manner. "Look, we're all sorry about this. Your brother went to get a Coke before being released on liberty. He stepped into the neighboring company's territory. Seven or eight new recruits beat him up. We are investigating the incident and I assure you the guilty parties will be punished."

"Beat up?" Suddenly Peter was in a rage as he visualized his brother being beaten. Of equal concern was the number of men it took to do it. Raving, Peter raced about the room throwing whatever he could get his hands on, overturning tables, and venting a sizzling stream of curses.

"D----- cowards can't fight one on one! H--- no! They've got to go seven on one! Where the h--- are they? They want a d--- fight, why don't you let them go seven on one with me?" he shouted at the lieutenant.

"Settle down or I'll have to call the MPs," warned the lieutenant.

"I don't give a s---!" Peter yelled back. But already his violence had exhausted itself. Taking a deep breath, he looked hard at the stone-faced lieutenant. "I want to see him. Where is he?"

"There is a naval hospital on this base. That is where you will find him."

Without another word Peter was gone. The hospital was not hard to find. Only a few miles farther along the same road, it lay nestled among the trees near a small lake.

Peter found his brother on a ward with twenty other beds. After getting clearance to visit, he entered the ward tentatively and approached the bed where his brother was sleeping, one eye swollen shut. There was a large black bruise under the other and his jaw looked disproportionate to his face. Peter was overwhelmed with emotions he had not felt in a long time, and he began to cry as he felt his brother's pain. Long, silent sobs accompanied the endless flow of tears.

His weeping had subsided when at last Jimmy woke up and saw Peter beside his bed. He tried to smile, but groaned when his mouth would not open. His broken jaw was wired shut. It was strange watching his brother try to talk using only his lips. But Jimmy managed.

Peter spent the afternoon beside him. They talked endlessly. It was good to see each other, even under these circumstances. They had a lot of catching up to do.

"How long are you going to have to stay in the hospital?" Peter asked.

"As long as my jaw is wired shut, I guess. About a month."

"Do you have to stay here?"

"On the base, but not in this building. I can go out on the grounds during the day."

"You have to stay on the base, though, huh?"

"Supposed to."

"Will they know if you don't?" Peter asked with a conspiratorial smile. He saw the light of comprehension go on in his brother's eyes as he tried to return the smile.

Without a further word it was decided. Peter would return tomorrow.

Once off the base, Peter began making plans. The first thing he had to do was get a car. Obviously, his brother was in no condition to ride behind him on the chopper.

As much as he loved that bike, Peter loved his brother more. He traded the bike for a 1961 Ford. It was cherry red with a black top. Although reluctant at first, the used-car dealer finally consented to an even trade. Peter was delighted.

Since he had brought no clothes with him, he drove around until he found a clothing outlet. It took only a few minutes to pick out a pair of blue jeans, tennis shoes, shirt, and baseball cap. He tucked his hair under the cap, and after he had trimmed his beard and changed clothes he looked like a different person. Now he was ready!

Off and on for the next four weeks, Peter drove his red and black Ford onto the base every morning and every afternoon. What the guards at the gate did not know was that his morning trip was to pick up his brother and the afternoon trip was to return him before he was missed. The guards did not know this because Peter transported his brother in the trunk of the car!

Off the base, they would drive to the beaches, only a short distance away, and the two of them would sunbathe for hours. Jimmy managed to sip beer through a straw. They talked and talked, spent hours getting to know one another again. Although he hated what had happened to his brother, Peter would not have traded those two weeks for anything in the world!

Taking a leave of absence from his job at the restaurant, Peter stayed near the base all the time his brother was hospitalized. He returned home only on Monday, Wednesday, and Friday evenings. On those nights he met Ed and they played chess and talked. Although Peter was no longer welcome in the classroom, there was little the school administration could do to keep him off the campus, particularly if they did not know he was there.

Peter was amazed that he had become so fond of Ed in such a short time. Married and with five daughters, Ed worked a construction job during the day and spent three nights a week on campus, attending classes, talking with the young students, and playing chess. Peter was surprised to discover the size of his following. Walking through the milling campus crowd with Ed was like going through a receiving line—he called most of the students by their first name! He seemed to know almost everyone—and they all liked him. Like Peter, they responded to his warmth and kindness. It took only a glance into those sensitive, knowing eyes to be assured of the wisdom and caring there.

"Chess is a lot like life," Ed had told Peter the first night they began the lessons. "The object is to win. To win, you must capture your opponent's king. And yet, in the playing of the game, there are many temptations that divert you from your objective, but seem worth pursuing nonetheless. The beginner will allow himself to be diverted from his objective, thus diverting vital thinking and energy into pursuits that have their rewards but may cost him the game."

Peter treasured the time he spent with Ed. Although he

lost the first hundred matches, the day finally came when he beat Ed for the first time. He was exhilarated!

"Congratulations, my friend!" Ed had offered excitedly. "You have won! At last the student has beaten the master and so is a student no more."

It was a strange new feeling for Peter to actually win at something—particularly against someone he admired and respected. He was amazed that Ed was as excited about losing as he was about winning! Losing to Ed had become a habit. Every match had begun with the expectation of a win for Ed and a loss for Peter. Breaking the habit, even in the midst of his celebration, made Peter feel uncomfortable. What else would change, now that he was no longer the student?

"How does it feel to lose for a change?" Peter asked with a smile.

"I know the feeling of defeat well, my friend! It is not new. What *is* new is seeing the glow of victory in your eyes!"

Peter was suddenly self-conscious. He felt awkward, as if he should apologize for having won.

"If you are going to play chess, Peter, you must learn the joy in defeat as well as victory. You will never win them all. At any given moment throughout your life, there will always be those beyond you and those behind you—those who play better and those who play not as well. You have won the game tonight. But that does not mean you will win our next game. If all you experience is joy when winning and grief when losing, then you will always be either a winner or a loser, neither of which brings peace. The loser will continually seek victory, while the victor will forever fear losing. As long as I can celebrate your victories and grieve your losses, then I have no fear of my own, do I?"

Although Peter was not sure he understood all Ed was trying to tell him that night, he was sure it was important. He carried the thought with him day after day, letting it play in his mind. Like a child with a new toy, he would grasp the thought and twist it and turn it to see its many sides and perspectives. Perhaps, in time, would come understanding.

Bobby, Peter's youngest brother, was to graduate from Marine Corps boot camp about a week before Jimmy was to be released from the naval hospital. Unlike Jimmy, Bobby had been so anxious to leave home that rather than attending high school another year, he had studied on his own and received a G.E.D. With diploma in hand, he had followed in Jimmy's footsteps and joined the Marines.

Once again, knowing no one else would be there to celebrate Bobby's graduation, Peter and Jimmy decided they would go. Sneaking Jimmy off the base was routine by now. Then they had to find some civilian clothes. He certainly would not be allowed through the guard gate wearing only hospital-issued pajamas and robe!

They sat in the stands along with the several hundred family members who had come to participate in the graduation exercises. Although they could not single Bobby out on the parade ground blanketed in dress blues, they knew he was there somewhere. One of those men was their brother. Already Peter felt closer to him and became even more anxious to see him. What a reunion it was going to be! The three of them together for the first time since Peter had been kicked out of the house!

They did not have long to wait. Soon a platoon of soldiers was marched into the visitors' waiting area and dismissed by the sergeant. It took his brothers only a second to spot Bobby among them. A second more and they were a pile of arms and legs on the ground in happy reunion. Laughing and wrestling, they were oblivious to the curious crowd around them. For a moment they were small boys again, clinging desperately together for the warmth and love that should have been theirs in a family.

"Private!" a deep, graveled voice barked.

Jimmy and Bobby both jumped to attention, leaving Peter sitting confused on the ground.

"Yes sir!" Bobby shouted, his eyes glued to some object straight ahead.

"What's going on here, Private?" the sergeant demanded, his face close to Bobby's.

"My brothers, sir!" Bobby answered.

"I see," said the sergeant, seemingly disappointed. He was on stage. Several hundred people were watching the scene.

"You military?" he turned to Jimmy.

Peter became alarmed when Jimmy did not answer right away. What if he were discovered AWOL from his base? He would really be in trouble then. Suddenly Peter was frightened for his brother.

"Naw, sergeant, I'm an ex," Jimmy answered at last, relaxing his posture. "I was discharged only last week."

Again the sergeant was disappointed. Returning his attention to Bobby, the only one still at full attention, the sergeant eyed him suspiciously for a long moment.

"Carry on, mister!" he barked at last and was gone.

The three sighed in relief. That was close. Watching his brothers respond to the sergeant created conflicting emotions in Peter. On the one hand, it made him angry to watch them being treated that way. But another part of him envied the fact that they were what he could never be—Marines. In Peter's mind at the time, Marines were the epitome of manliness. They had become *real* men. He was just a biker. A worm. The epitome of low-life. Experiencing the contrast, Peter felt the difference between them. Jimmy and Bobby had something in common he could never be a part of. At that moment, he felt ashamed and inadequate in their presence. Even worse, for the first time in his life, he felt a stranger in his brothers' world.

The three spent the rest of the afternoon visiting and talking under a tree in the picnic area roped off for the occasion. Bobby would not get leave until he had completed advanced infantry training. He was scheduled to be transported there that afternoon. Peter listened quietly as his brothers compared experiences from boot camp and made plans to see each other on the base.

It was hard to leave at the appointed hour. Watching the platoon re-form and march off only increased the shame and helplessness Peter already felt. He loved his brothers so much! He would do anything for them! How he wished he could share their lives as military men.

After returning Jimmy to the hospital, Peter drove home. The reunion with his brothers had created such a powerful emotional response and stirred up so many unfamiliar feelings, he felt he had to get away for a while. As it turned out, Jimmy was dismissed from the hospital early and promptly shipped to his first duty station in another part of the country. It would be a long while before he would see Jimmy again.

But he saw Bobby only a few weeks later at graduation from advanced infantry training. Peter was sitting in the visitors' parking lot with all the other guests, waiting for Bobby. Only moments before the scheduled dismissal for liberty, word came that all leaves had been cancelled. Jane Fonda was leading a war-protest rally and thousands of peace-loving hippies were surrounding the base with the intention of invading it. The base was being put on military alert and closed to all outsiders. With a show of genuine regret, the lieutenant asked the waiting families to leave as quickly and in as orderly a fashion as possible

"Lieutenant?" Peter approached the officer tentatively.

"Yes?" he responded, eyeing Peter curiously.

"My brother was scheduled to go on leave today with the others. He has another brother in the Marine Corps who is shipping out for Vietnam in a couple of days. If he can't come home with me now, he may never see his brother again. Is there anything I can do to get him home?" Peter asked, his voice sincere and pleading.

For a long time the lieutenant did not answer. He just continued to look at Peter with eyes that seemed indecisive.

"What is the private's name?" he asked at last.

Peter told him.

"Wait here," he said and disappeared into the duty hut.

The parking lot still had not been totally cleared when down the hill a soldier in full dress uniform came running, waving his arms and shouting at the top of his lungs.

"Am I ever glad to see you!" he yelled as he scrambled into the car. "Hurry! Let's get out of there before they change their minds! By the way, how did you manage to get me out of there?"

Bobby was the only man to get leave. Peter would do anything for his brothers.

Nine

Since that fateful night several months ago when he had sat at the foot of the cross overlooking the city, Peter had decided to go to school. Education, he believed, was the key that would unlock the prison of his history. Perhaps he could not only train his mind, but also learn to control it as he sought to diminish his childhood while increasing the potential of his future.

But already he had failed at school. The school officials had banned him from the classrooms. After weeks of thinking about it, Peter was still confused. He wanted to be in school. But how? How can you make a person or institution want you when they have already made it clear they want nothing more to do with you? Getting nowhere in his own thinking, Peter at last decided to talk to Ed.

It was a warm summer evening. The campus was alive with activity as students made their way to and from class, stopping to talk and laugh in small clusters along the way. Peter envied them as one might envy the talent of a concert pianist, knowing full well the limits of one's own abilities. But in the end, he rationalized, it really did not matter. He had been on the outside looking in for so long that he would lose all perspective, should that change.

"What's happenin', brother?" Ed's soft, melodious voice

came out of the darkness as he approached the table where Peter sat waiting.

"It's my turn to be white, is it not?" he asked as he sat down.

After setting up the board, Ed moved his king's pawn to king four to open. The game progressed through ten moves before either of them spoke.

"When are you going to get back into school?" Ed asked, eyeing him curiously. For a moment Peter was caught off guard, as though Ed had read his mind.

"Get back in school?" he mimicked at last.

"You are coming back, aren't you?"

"Do you think I can?"

"Have you tried?"

"No. They kicked me out," Peter added in self-defense.

"I know. Does that mean you can't come back?" Ed pressed on.

"I don't know." This was a new thought for Peter. "I guess I assumed they wouldn't want me back."

"Why did you assume they would not let you back, instead of assuming that they would?"

"I don't understand." Peter dodged the question, giving his mind time to explore its possibilities.

"When you sat down here to play this game of chess," Ed began, looking directly at Peter, "did you assume that you would win or that you would lose?"

"Well, I don't know. I guess I didn't think about it."

"Sure you did!" exclaimed Ed. "Would you play a game of chess against a man you knew without a doubt was going to beat you?"

Peter thought about this for a moment.

"No, I guess not," he answered. "Why bother!"

"But you do bother, don't you? You do sit down here and play chess. Three times a week in fact. You would not do that if you did not believe that you had a chance to beat me, to win. Without that belief, you would never even try, would you?"

"I see what you mean!" exclaimed Peter, beginning to become excited.

106

"Don't you see that the limit of a man is his imagination?" Ed continued, as though to drive home his point. "If he can imagine it, then it is possible! No matter what it is. Even getting back into school. Where you and I make our mistake is that we assume the worst, and so never even try. But how can a door open without someone turning the handle? The only reason you are not back in school is you!"

In the ensuing silence, Ed returned his concentration to the game. But Peter's thoughts were elsewhere. He was trying to understand the new feeling of optimism that had suddenly taken hold of him.

"It's your move," Ed had to remind him.

Peter moved. Ed smiled and sat back. Lighting a cigarette, he offered Peter one as well.

"Life, my friend," Ed began softly, "is like my next move. I have three choices. I can move my rook. This would result in your being able to capture my knight and so gain an advantage over me. Or I can capture your bishop with my own and gain an advantage over you. Or I could just possibly move my queen to your king's bishop two for a checkmate and a win!"

Shocked, Peter riveted his eyes to the board. It took only a few moments to see that Ed was right. It was mate in one! The match was Ed's if he wanted it.

"And naturally you will choose the mate move," Peter sighed deeply in resignation.

"Which of the three moves I choose to make will depend, of course, on why I am playing the game, will it not? If I am playing to lose, I will make the move that will give you the advantage. If I am playing to tease and torment, I will make the move that will give me the advantage. But if I am playing to win, I will go for the kill. Checkmate!" he concluded with a flourish.

Peter groaned. He hated to lose. But what he learned in this defeat concerned a great deal more than chess. For the first time, Peter began to visualize life as an elaborate and sophisticated game of chess.

"Always go for the win, my friend," Ed concluded, still watching Peter closely through the curtain of smoke that hung between them. "It's your move!"

. . .

Two weeks later Peter was standing in the office of the dean of admissions. His application for readmission was being decided by the dean himself.

"How badly do you want an education, young man?" the dean asked from behind his large desk. His steady blue eyes seemed to be measuring every inch of Peter.

"I want it bad," Peter mumbled, afraid to meet the man's gaze.

"You are a Saint, aren't you?" he probed further. "How important to you is that?"

"They are all I've got!" Peter exclaimed, suddenly defensive. "They are like my family."

"I see," the man said and slumped into deep thought. Peter waited nervously for the rejection he was sure would come. Although he was trying desperately to stay positive, life had taught him not to expect too much. But at least he was trying! After a moment more, the dean spoke again.

"Do you want an education badly enough to leave your colors at home?" he asked.

"Yeah, I can do that. Sure, I don't have to wear my colors." For a moment Peter got excited. That was a small price to pay. Maybe he could do it after all.

"Do you want an education badly enough to cut your hair and shave your beard?"

The question stung Peter and crushed the flicker of hope. Already he had given up his bike for a car. And he was willing to not wear his colors on campus. But cut his hair? And shave off his beard? He would not even *look* like a biker then! He would look like everybody else. But isn't that what you want? his mind asked. No, no, no! I don't want to *look* like everybody else. I just want to *be* like everybody else! But how can you be like them if you don't look like them? his mind battled on.

"Well, son, what do you think?" the dean broke into his thoughts. "Are your hair and beard more important than your education?"

Seconds passed into minutes as Peter contemplated his choice. As badly as he wanted to be back in school, the dean was tampering with his identity. The possibility of having to deny himself in order to fulfill himself had not occurred to him. Why can't people just leave me alone? he moaned to himself. Why can't they just accept me the way I am? Although full of self-pity, his greatest battle was to control his simmering anger as part of him resisted the authority that was forcing him to change. Despairing, he was torn with tumultuous thoughts and conflicting emotions. At last a voice came to him, soft and clear: "What choice you make will depend on why you are playing the game. Go for the win!"

"Will you let me back in school if I do what you want?" he asked at last.

"All right. Here's the deal. I can't tell you how to dress, when to shave, or how to wear your hair. But given your record, I don't have to let you back on the campus, either. But we are in the education business. We want to encourage young people such as yourself to get an education. But I need to know that you mean business this time. Cutting your hair and shaving would show me just how serious you are. You do that, and I will readmit you to this school—on probation. What that means is that just one more incident with a teacher, and you're gone for good. It also means that should another fight occur between you and a fellow student on this campus, you will not just get up and walk away. We will call the police and it will be handled through the criminal justice system. And you will stay on probation until I let you off. Do I make myself clear?"

"Yes," Peter answered sullenly.

"Violence is the most primitive and barbaric form of human interaction," the dean went on as though thinking out loud. "Animals fight. Civilized human beings have a brain that both compels and inspires them to peaceful, nonviolent resolutions." The dean returned his direct gaze to Peter and watched him for a long moment before continuing. "That's the deal, son. You go home and think about it. Registration for next semester starts Thursday. Drop by my office that morning if you decide this is what you want."

Peter did not spend the next couple of days trying to decide what to do, but trying to deal with the anger building up and spilling over at *having* to do it. He had already made his decision while sitting in the dean's office. In the end he went to a rock concert on the beach with the Saints. The partying started the night before and ended the morning after the concert. Peter threw himself with reckless abandon into the festivities, his drugged mind senseless to possible consequences. At one point he even climbed on stage, took the microphone, and poured out his rage in an antiauthoritarian, antisystem monologue that drew cheers even from portions of the crowd gathered only to hear the music. Perhaps it was his farewell gesture. Or maybe it was his way of suffering—bearing the pain of change.

Bleary-eyed and exhausted Thursday morning, Peter managed to reach the dean's office just as the man was about to leave. They met in the outer office. The dean's eyes glanced over him and beyond without recognition as he started out the door.

"Dean!" Peter almost shouted before the man could get away.

"Yes?" The dean paused, now looking hard at Peter. "No, it can't be! Peter, this is incredible! Except for your bloodshot eyes, you look like a real human being!"

Extremely embarrassed and self-conscious, Peter shuffled from one foot to the other, not knowing how to respond. He just wanted to get his readmit card and get out.

"I came to register for classes," he mumbled.

"So I see, so I see! I just can't get over how different you look," the man continued unheeded. "Well, come on into my office for a minute. I have what I think might be a surprise for you. Miss Stevens," he said as he paused by the secretary's desk, "please call Dr. Evans and inform him I will be late for the meeting."

"A surprise?" Peter was both curious and concerned. What could the dean possibly mean? He did not have to wait long to find out.

"I thought you might be back, Peter, and I'm glad you are," he spoke quickly without sitting down. "Now, first things first. Here is your readmit card. I've already signed it. All you need do is take it to the registrar's office. They will give you everything you need to register for classes. OK?"

"OK. Thanks." Peter moved to leave.

"Sit still. I'm not finished yet. Do you know what a work-study program is?" he asked, polishing the lenses of his glasses.

"No."

"Well, it's a program that allows students with financial need to work at jobs in the community while going to school. They not only get paid for the work, but earn academic credit as well. It is a way we have devised to help certain promising young people who otherwise would not be able to afford an education." The man paused to catch his breath. "Would you be interested in this program?"

"You mean for me?" Peter was surprised. Why would the dean want to help him? Suddenly Peter was suspicious. Helping hands had been few and far between. And when they were offered, they usually had a price tag of some sort tucked neatly out of sight in one of the cuffs.

"Yes, for you. There is a school here in town that has asked us for a student to work as a teacher's aide for this year. It's an elementary school with a student population of around eight hundred. And," he paused as he studied Peter for a reaction, "it's a ghetto school with a lot of racial tension. You were the first one I thought of when the request came across my desk. What do you think?"

"You mean you are offering me that job?" Peter asked incredulously, not daring to believe what he was hearing.

"Well, no, I can't offer you the job. But I can arrange an interview for you and personally recommend you to the principal."

"Why me?" Peter eyed the dean suspiciously, still waiting for the catch.

The dean moved slowly to the window and seemed to lose himself in the view. After a while, Peter began to wonder if the man had forgotten he was still in the room. But then the dean spoke.

"When I was a boy—about eight, I guess—my father died. Car accident. My mother had to go to work to support the four of us kids. But she didn't make much as a waitress, so we were hungry a lot. I ran away, thinking like kids do sometimes that it would be easier for her if she had one less mouth to feed and that maybe I could find a job somewhere and send Mother the money. Naturally I didn't make it very far. About eight blocks, to be exact. That's where Charlie Chan found me. They called him Charlie Chan because he looked oriental, wore his hair in a pony tail, and had one of those Fu Manchu mustaches, know what I mean?" he asked, though not turning to Peter.

"Anyway, he took me in, fed me, and let me sleep at his place. I told him what I was doing and why. The next day he took me home and asked my mother if he could drop by to see me from time to time. She said it was all right, so he did. Once a week for two years he came by. Every time he did he would bring a bag of groceries, and sometimes Mother would find a couple of ten or twenty dollar bills rolled together in the egg carton. And he would always take me to a movie, or to the park, or just to ride around on his bike. You see, Charlie Chan was a biker. I don't know what Mother would have done without his help."

"What ever happened to him?" Peter asked curiously.

"He was killed in a street fight," the dean answered

unemotionally, turning back to look at Peter. "There is a kid somewhere in that ghetto school who needs you."

Peter was totally overwhelmed. The thought that anyone, let alone a child, needed him was more than he dared hope for. He had been an outcast, living on the fringes of civilized life so long that it was hard to imagine himself in any other role. Although the idea intrigued him, it also frightened him.

"What do you say?" pressed the dean. "You want to give it a shot?"

"All right. Just tell me what I need to do," Peter answered.

"Good. My office will be in touch with you after we have set up the interview. Should be a couple of weeks at the most."

"Great!" Peter exclaimed and stood up. This was becoming more than he could handle. Overflowing with feelings he did not want to reveal, he was anxious to go some place where he could be alone to think about everything. It was all happening so fast! Fighting the temptation to bolt headlong out of the building, Peter offered his hand to the dean, a gesture he had always rejected as a symbol of oppression, rather than goodwill.

"By the way," the dean added, taking Peter's hand, "There is a five hundred dollar grant from the school waiting for you at the financial aid window. Just a little help to get you started."

Returning to the same rock jetty where he had sat only a couple of years before, Peter spent the rest of that day in his private corner of the universe. The earth, the sea, and the sky enveloped him in their meeting, and there he unraveled the mysteries of the morning.

As before, Peter cried out his pain among the rocks, his tears washed away in an ocean far greater than they. But it was a different pain this time. It was the pain that comes when food first touches a stomach that has gone hungry for days and days. Or the pain that comes when a frozen heart is first touched by a thawing warmth.

For whatever reason, the dean had reached beyond his own life and responsibilities to touch the life of Peter. Sitting now alone in the midst of his world, Peter knew he would never again be the same.

Ten

Peter was accepted into the work-study program. He would work as a teacher's aide at the elmentary school on Mondays, Wednesdays, and Fridays while taking classes the other two days and at night. It was going to be a busy schedule. But he liked that. It would make him feel as though he were actually accomplishing something.

Though excited by the changes that seemed to be occurring in his life, Peter was constantly haunted by his feelings of inadequacy and fear of failure. At times those feelings became so intense, it was all he could do to keep himself from abandoning the effort altogether. He just wanted to run and hide where no one could find him, where he would not need to measure up or be what he thought others wanted him to be. There were times when only one thing stood between him and headlong flight—Ed.

"I can't make it, man!" Peter blurted out one evening. For an hour he had sat across the table from Ed, absentmindedly playing chess. Absorbed in his own thoughts, he had not noticed that Ed, too, was strangely quiet.

"Make what?" Ed asked softly as he looked up from the game.

"Everything!" Peter exclaimed. "School, the job at the school, grades—h--- man, everything that's coming up! You know as well as I do that they'll find out sooner or later!"

"Find out about what?"

"Me, man, me! I'm trash! H---, you don't send trash to

school or give it a job working with kids. You pile it in a corner and forget it!" Peter moaned in dismay.

Ed watched the agitated Peter for a long moment.

"Tell me something," he said at last. "What's the difference between trash and treasure?"

"I don't know, man. I've never thought about it."

"Well, think about it!" directed Ed. "You're so convinced you are trash that you at least ought to know what it is."

"All right. Trash is bad and unwanted. Treasure is good and wanted."

"Maybe *your* trash, but not *mine!*" exclaimed Ed.

"What the h--- are you talking about, man!" Peter was beginning to get irritated. "Come on. Don't play games with me!"

"Look, Peter!" Ed became intense. He leaned forward to look directly into Peter's eyes. "There is an equal portion of good and bad in all things—and in all people. Which we see depends on what we are looking for and why we are looking for it! Don't you see? What is important is how we see something and how we use it. Take drugs. They can be used to kill pain, and that is good. Or they can be used to blow a mind, and that is bad. Right? Or this pencil," Ed continued feverishly, brandishing one in his hand. "I can use it as an instrument of communication between you and me—which is good; or I can poke your eye out with it—which is bad. And the same is true for everything else. Everything. Even a pile of trash like you!" he concluded with a smile.

Peter was shocked. This was a totally new thought. He had been raised to believe something was wrong with him, that he was bad. That was why his parents had not wanted him, nor had all the foster parents he had lived with. And that was why his adopted parents had to beat him.

Believing for almost twenty years that he was an inherently bad and evil person made it all the more difficult for him to accept what Ed was telling him. Was it possible some aspect of him was good? But how could good and bad exist in the same person, or object? How could a person be both at the same time? People were either good or bad, he thought.

"That's heavy, man," Peter acknowledged with a sigh. "I'll be thinking about that for a long time."

"Now what is this business about not making it?" Ed asked.

"I don't know, man. I just feel I'm going to screw up royally and then people are going to be mad at me, and I'm going to end up having to quit school and the job. You know—like I'm living in a pipe dream, trying to be something I'm not. It's like I'm waitin' for the final judgment, knowin' full well what it's goin' to be."

"Don't you know that in the end there is only one judge and jury, and you are it? The world and other people can have only what you choose to give them. If you give them your fear and weakness, then that is all of you they will ever know. Why not give them your love and strength? You cast a little love upon the masses, and watch what happens! It's like water on a desert. It makes possible the life that quickly consumes it. There are people who desperately need the love you have to share, Peter. Have the courage to reach beyond your own existence to touch another life! The amazing thing is, if you do, you will find that in your touching, you yourself will be touched. And both of you will be the better for it."

Overwhelmed by so much so quickly, Peter sat listening in undisguised admiration. He wanted Ed to go on and on. But Ed stopped talking, sat back, and lit a cigarette.

"Heavy, huh?" he asked through a pall of smoke.

"Yeah," Peter answered. "Thanks."

"No need for thanks. I care." After a moment of silence as they studied the board between them to determine their next moves, Ed spoke again. "Listen, Peter. This will have to be our last match."

"Last match?" Peter was confused.

"I'm afraid so. The heat is on. The word is on the street that I hit on an undercover narc and an indictment willl come down in a couple of days. I hear it's part of a big bust.

Anyway, I've got to pack up and get out while I'm still free to move around."

"Where will you go?" Peter asked in dismay. The thought of losing this new friend was almost more than he could bear. His mind still had not accepted the full meaning of what Ed was saying.

"The old lady has been wanting to homestead somewhere. I hear there is land still available in certain wilderness parts of Canada. Guess we'll go there and see if we can get lost. Live off the land, you know. The kids will like that."

"Will you write, or at least let me know where you are?"

"Can't. We'll just have to disappear and start over again. Guess I'll have to go back to the computer for my chess until one of my kids is old enough to learn."

That night when Peter watched Ed disappear into the darkness, knowing he probably would never see him again, he became fully aware of how important Ed had become to him. Crushed and lonely, he went on a binge. Loading himself with drugs and alcohol, he drove around town looking for someone or something to relieve the pain. The more he drove, the more frightened he became. What was he going to do without Ed to talk to?

After what seemed like hours of wandering, he found himself at a familiar place. The beach. He thought of the hours he had spent walking its length or sitting alone among its rocks, trying to overcome the pain and torment that seemed so much a part of his life; the times he had come here looking for answers to endless questions that gave him no peace. Or just to get away from everything over which he had no control. Like now. Michael was dead. Ed was gone. The dreams about his mother and sister seemed to be growing in frequency and intensity. His classes and grades. And the job at the school where he would be having a direct impact upon the lives of children. What was he going to do? Everything had been so simple before all the changes started. Why did he have to change? Why did he have to *want* to change?

Totally overwhelmed, Peter began to sob, releasing all his

emotions. For a moment he was a child again, crying out his fear, frustration, and loneliness to these same rocks. But only for a moment.

"Are you all right?" asked a feminine voice behind him.

Caught totally by surprise, Peter almost fell off the rock as he spun around toward the voice. Even through the mist of tears he could see her in the dim light. She was wearing an ankle-length dress with a white shawl around her shoulders. From where Peter was sitting, she looked very tall. The length of her hair made her seem even taller. There was concern in her eyes as she leaned slightly forward to get a better look at him in the shadows. Peter sat speechless, staring as though stunned by a vision.

"Are you all right?" she asked again softly, taking a step closer.

Her voice snapped Peter out of his trance, confirming her reality to his doubting senses.

"Yeah, yeah," he was able to mumble at last. "I'm all right."

"You were crying," she said matter-of-factly. "Is something wrong?"

Peter looked hard at the girl. She was alone. He could not see a companion anywhere, and yet she did not seem afraid of him. Why not? Most females would not even stop to talk to him during broad daylight, let alone at night alone on a semidark beach.

"What are you doing out here?" he asked.

"Taking a walk before I go home," she answered. "I love the beach. It's so calming and soothing. Particularly at night. You come here often?"

"No," he lied, terribly aware not only of being alone in a romantic place popular with couples, but also of the fact that she had caught him crying like a baby. He was embarrassed on both counts.

She hesitated as though suddenly unsure of herself.

"Well, if you're sure you are all right, I guess I'll go on," she said lightly and started away.

"Don't go! Please!" Peter blurted without thinking.

"What?" She paused.

"I mean, would you mind if I walked with you a little way?" he mumbled nervously, afraid she would get the wrong idea and reject him. Suddenly he could not stand the thought of being alone for another second. Somehow he had to find a way to keep her with him a while longer. At least until he felt better.

She seemed to be thinking.

"I guess it will be all right," she said at last. "I was getting a little lonely myself. Come on."

Peter was up in a flash. Like a moth around a light on a summer night, he hovered around her as they walked, his every sense tuned to her, afraid he would do or say something to make her leave.

For a long time they walked along the edge of the surf in silence. Occasionally they would observe how good the mist felt on their faces, or how beautifully the moon was reflected on the water, or how much they loved the beach. Although he could smell her perfume, he dared not look at her for fear she would vanish from his sight. It felt so good to be with her. So peaceful. Though neither seemed to have much to say, the silence was not awkward. On the contrary, it seemed to take on a special meaning as something they shared together.

They were nearing the parking lot when she spoke again.

"Something was bothering you back there. Can I help?" she asked with genuine concern. "I can at least listen, if that would help."

He really did not want to talk about it or admit that he had been crying. In the end, he did, but only because he could think of no other way to keep her with him a while longer. He talked mostly about his dreams of his mother and sister.

"You must love them a lot," she observed when he finished.

"I don't know. I've never thought about it," he answered, suddenly curious himself. Did he love them? How could he not? After all, they were his mother and sister. But then, how could he love them? He did not even know them! How do you love someone you probably would not recognize if you met on the street? These and a thousand other thoughts went racing through his mind.

"Maybe I don't know how to love them. Maybe what I love is the idea of them. Suppose?"

"I can understand that. You love them as you remember them, which may not be the way they are today at all!"

"Yeah, that's it!" he agreed.

"Well, when are you going to go find them?" she asked.

The fact that she naturally assumed he would try to find his lost family did not escape Peter.

"I don't know where to look," he answered.

"You will find them someday," she assured him. "You'll see!"

With these final words she stepped close to Peter and hugged him gently, her cheek lightly brushing his. It felt so soft and cool. The touch of her hair sent a small tickling sensation racing through his body. With a last glance at him, she stepped into her car and was gone.

It was not until the tail lights were out of sight that Peter realized he did not even know her name. How could he be such a fool as to let her get away? He kicked himself. The least he could have done was get her phone number.

Slowly the anger subsided and Peter found himself once again alone on the beach with only his memory of the girl as his companion. Still frustrated and feeling totally helpless, he stripped off his clothes and went for a swim in the dark and pounding surf. The water was refreshing and helped clear his thoughts.

For a moment he was tempted to swim out beyond the breakers and white water—out into that dark expanse of water as far as he could go until he could no longer stay afloat. How easy it would be, he thought, to just keep swimming until at last he could swim no more. It would all be over then. He would not hurt anymore. Besides, what did he have to live for? His brothers were in the service and no longer needed him. It was just him. And that certainly was not much. Not enough to keep fighting for, anyway.

But something made him swim back to shore. Maybe it was the hope somewhere deep in the recesses of his mind that he would meet the girl again someday, somewhere. Or maybe it was just that he had survived too much too long to give up now.

"Go for the win!" Ed had said.

"How?" screamed Peter's tormented soul.

"There is only one way," the priest had assured him.

That's it! The priest. He had the answer. Peter vowed then to visit the priest again as soon as he could. If the priest had the answer, then he wanted it. Knowing his next move made him feel better.

He put on his undershorts and lay on the sand to rest. Lighting a cigarette, he enjoyed the moment of silent communion with the earth, sea, and sky around him.

Ready to leave, he threw his clothes in the back seat of the car. He took a case of beer out of the trunk, set it on the seat beside him and, still dressed only in his boxer shorts, drove toward town. Holding a can of beer between his thighs, he popped the top. With the radio blaring rock and roll, he drank deeply and began dragging Main Street along with the other Saturday night draggers.

Moving twenty miles below the speed limit, slow enough to frustrate any driver seriously trying to get somewhere, the line of cars snaked its way two abreast down the main street. Peter watched with amusement as the carload of high school girls in front of him stopped at a red light, then exploded with opening doors and dashing people as they went through a Chinese fire drill. Peter took the opportunity to look over each girl in that car as well as those in the cars around him. Although he did not want to admit it, he was looking for the girl on the beach. Every face was her face until he could get a good look at it. It was going to be a long night.

The line of cars did not move forward when the light turned green. It took only a moment for horns to begin blowing their impatience. The problem seemed to be with the car in front of the girls in front of Peter. By leaning halfway out the window, he saw that the group of boys in that car had automobile parts scattered all over the street in both lanes. From all appearances they were working on the engine in the middle of the street, and having a good time doing it.

Knowing the line would not be moving for quite a while, depending on how soon the police arrived to urge the would-be mechanics on their way, Peter decided to go around them. When the traffic coming from the opposite direction was clear, he jerked his car out of line and, with a squeal of tires, raced past the obstruction. He did not see the policeman on the side street. But the policeman saw him. Suddenly there were red lights flashing in his rear-view mirror.

Disgusted, Peter pulled over. Still wearing only his undershorts, he made no effort to get out. The officer approached him cautiously from the rear and asked to see his license, then waited patiently while Peter dug through his clothes in the back seat for his wallet.

The officer told Peter to get out of the car to hand him the license. As he did so, he noticed the traffic was moving again. Standing in the street, obviously having been pulled over, and wearing only his undershorts, Peter soon became the center of catcalls and whistles. After trying to explain to the officer why he was in his underwear and why he had been racing down the wrong side of the street, Peter was made to pour out the contents of all twenty-three cans of undrunk beer.

The officer issued a traffic ticket with four violations totaling over a hundred dollars, then laughed and sent Peter on his way with a suggestion that he go straight home.

Peter's mistake was in not waiting until the man was well past before he flashed the obscene gesture. Peter did not sleep in his own bed that night. Nor for the next two nights. Instead, he was lodged unceremoniously in the city jail on DUI charges. The sad part was that he did not mind.

Eleven

A hush fell as Peter stepped through the door. For a moment a hundred suspicious and threatening eyes were upon him. Recognizing him for one of their own, most of the occupants returned to what they were doing.

"It's just Mr. Clean!" announced a voice.

"Hey, wha's happenin', Professor?" another called from a darkened corner.

Peter ignored the calls and moved on into the room. A young girl with waist-length blond hair was standing on the bar taking off her clothes and dancing to music that blared from a nearby juke box. Peter could tell by her movements and her smile that she was stoned out of her mind. Some men were gathered around the girl, cheering, playing cards. Still others were huddled around two pool tables in the rear of the lounge, where money was being exchanged in attempts to beat the club sharpshooter at his own game. The room was filled with cigarette smoke and the smell of burning marijuana. Slowly Peter made his way to the open end of the bar. He noticed the crowd included several of the Saints' women scattered among the men.

"Beer," he ordered in response to the bartender's questioning look.

"Dollar," stated the man. He placed the bottle on the bar in front of Peter and, with a swift and practiced move, took off the cap with the opener fastened to a chain securely attached to his belt.

"Where's Sheik?" Peter asked before the man got away.

"In the back. He's got company."

"What kind of company?"

"How the h--- should I know?" the man barked and moved quickly away.

It had been several days since Peter was last in the Den—home base of the Saints—not since he had cut his hair and shaved his beard. Although he had never felt totally at ease with all the Saints, it was a new feeling to seem so different from them. He wondered how just looking different could make him feel so uncomfortable. Something had changed. Was it he? Or them? Peter could not tell, but he could certainly feel the change as he made his way through the crowd toward the back of the room.

Peter could see Sheik in the last booth along the wall. He was talking to someone across from him. Again Peter marveled at the man. Six feet tall and muscular, he had olive skin and black hair that streamed in waves across his shoulders and down his back. His white teeth stood out in sharp contrast when he smiled. His dark eyes were constantly moving, dancing with light and laughter or searching out an enemy with deadly seriousness. Peter had learned he was the son of an Arab sheik who owned a large ranch in a neighboring state. Most of his life had been spent in the United States, although his father constantly traveled back and forth between the two countries. Peter was told that as a junior in high school, Sheik had been an all-American football player, with several major colleges already standing in line to recruit him. Then during his senior year . . . a suicide attempt, the stay in the mental hospital, his father's refusal to visit him there, then his discharge from the hospital back into the family. But he had chosen to live on the street and forfeit his last year of high school rather than live under the same roof with his father.

As Peter neared the booth, a woman stood up to leave. He recognized her as the manager of The Palace, one of the three massage parlors owned and operated by the Saints. Like some other apparently legitimate businesses, it was a front for prostitution, pornography, and drug trafficking.

"I've got to have more girls," she was saying as she picked up her purse. "Can you rotate a few out of another region? I can't keep up with business without more help."

"We'll see, baby, we'll see," Sheik answered with a smile.

"What about the b---- doing her thing on the bar? Why can't I have her?"

124

"I've got plans for her," he said as he looked at Peter approaching the table. "But if it doesn't work out, then she's yours. How's that?"

"How long?" she asked.

"Tomorrow, baby. I'll know by tomorrow."

The woman left. Peter took her place in the booth opposite Sheik.

"What's happenin', my man?" Sheik grinned.

"Word got to me you wanted to see me," Peter answered as he lit a cigarette. He would have offered one, but he knew Sheik didn't smoke, drink, or do drugs. The man was clean.

"Yeah, guess I did." He eyed Peter through the smoke. "How long you been a Saint?"

"Over two years. Why?"

"You like it?"

"Sure, man. Why wouldn't I?"

"Then why are you wanting to move out of the pad?" Sheik asked.

During his entire life with the bikers, Peter had been living in a two-bedroom apartment with several other club members. After being reaccepted into college, he had announced his intention of finding a place of his own. Obviously word had gotten back to Sheik.

"It's too crowded and noisy. I can't study there," Peter answered honestly.

"Study? You planning on going to school or something?"

"I've already been accepted."

Sheik seemed to think about this before he spoke again. He sat very still, his face inscrutable. Peter could not tell what he was thinking. Only his eyes moved.

"Tell me something, man." He finally spoke, leaning closer to Peter as though to emphasize his words. "All the time I've known you, I've never seen you with a chick. Why is that?"

Suddenly Peter was defensive. The shift in the conversation to the subject of his masculinity caught him by surprise.

"What do you mean?" he asked, buying time to think.

"Just what I said, man. Some of the guys seem to think you don't like girls. That so?"

"That's b--- s---, man!" Peter exploded. "You've known me long enough to know that's not true!"

"Yeah?"

"Yeah, d-----!"

"What about her?" Sheik continued, indicating the naked girl still dancing on the bar. "You like her?"

"She looks all right," he answered, still stinging from the earlier implication.

"You want her?" he asked, still watching Peter closely.

"What the h--- for, man? She's a w----!" Peter answered with disgust.

"No she's not, man. She's a virgie. Sixteen-year-old runaway from back East. Joker picked her up yesterday near the bus station. She's clean, man," Sheik assured him. "And she's all yours if you want her."

Peter lit another cigarette and watched Sheik suspiciously. What was he up to? he wondered. Why this sudden interest?

"Why me?" Peter asked.

"Because I like you, man," Sheik answered lightly with one of his dazzling grins. "And because I want you to have the best."

"Why?" Peter pressed.

"Well, let's put it this way," he answered after a moment. "Iron Man was busted last week. Looks like he'll do some time. That leaves a vacancy in the leadership. I want you to plug the hole, man. I take care of my heads. They get the best. You will, too. Just like the others. Nothing but the best. Like her. And others after her. Consider it a promotion." He smiled again.

To an outsider it sounded like a command. To most others it would have been. But Peter knew that in his case it was an invitation, though the consequences could be just as serious if he refused.

"Why me?" he asked again.

"You're smart," Sheik acknowledged. "And angry. I like

126

that. Besides, you were kicked around so much as a kid, I know I can trust you. You would never stab me in the back. If you were going to stab me, you would come at me face to face."

It was a compliment. And a confession of vulnerability. It was an invitation to become one of the chosen few who maintained an intimate relationship with their leader. Peter was flattered. A part of him was intrigued by the thought. For long moments he turned the possibilities over in his mind. What it would mean to be envied by others, to become a trusted and loyal lieutenant of one of the most powerful club leaders in the country. What power he would have at last! And respect. He would really be somebody then!

Peter had known this moment would come—that sooner or later he would have to make a final decision. It was a choice between being a biker and all it had to offer, and going straight. He knew what he had with the bikers; it was concrete and immediate. There were no guarantees that he would ever have anything in the straight world. It was a choice between sure acceptance and approval, and taking the risk of more failure and rejection.

As he sat alone in his moment of decision under the watchful eye of his mentor, Peter's mind was flooded with endless voices:

"I want you to fill the vacancy . . . "

"Go in peace to love and serve the Lord . . . "

"You'll have nothing but the best . . . "

"Go for the win . . . "

"There is a kid out there who needs you . . . "

"He sent his Son to show you the way . . . "

"You can have her and anything else you want . . . "

The voices went on and on until they became a roar in his mind. How desperately he wanted to be accepted, wanted to have a place among others. That is what Sheik was offering him. And wealth and power on top of that!

A decision began to crystallize. He would accept the invitation and abandon his plans to attend school. Then suddenly a fight erupted between two notoriously antagonistic club women who had been watching the pool matches. What started the fight was anybody's guess.

Peter's alarm turned to disgust as he watched the women on the floor, clawing and kicking at each other in a twisted pile of hair and torn clothing. He was even more disgusted by the men, who stood around in a circle cheering them on, taking bets on who would win, how long it would last, and which would lose her top first.

Like pit dogs, the women tore at each other viciously amid screams and curses. Peter knew from experience that they would continue, battered and bloodied, until one was beaten into submission or they both dropped from exhaustion. The men would see to it. It made Peter want to vomit.

It was then he heard her voice again. Soft and gentle. A caressing whisper echoing a love through years of yearning and desperate seeking. So different from the voices around him screaming in sordid pain and pleasure. Yet it was more clear than any he had ever heard. It was his mother's voice, singing. "Jesus loves me, this I know, for the Bible tells me so . . ."

There was an urgency in her voice. She was trying to tell him something. Something important. As he listened and once again felt the peace her voice always brought, Peter knew what he had to do. No longer was there any temptation. All doubt was gone.

"Man, I've got to get out of here!" he muttered under his breath. He got up and strode to the door.

Sheik followed him outside. Leaning against the wall below the flashing neon light, the men breathed deep of the cool, fresh air and were silent for a long time. Nervously, Peter lit another cigarette as he fought against the fear that threatened him. At last he could speak.

"Look, man! I've lived with that kind of s--- all my life. Being treated like a piece of worthless trash. Nobody caring whether you were beaten to death or not. Man, I just can't live like that anymore!" He pleaded desperately.

For a long time Sheik did not answer. Only the roars and cheers of the crowd inside broke the stillness around them. "So, " he spoke finally in a whisper. "You want to go to school."

"Man, I've got to! Don't you see? It's the only way I can survive!"

"Survive? What the h--- you talking to me about survival for, man?" Sheik screamed in a sudden burst of anger. "You think you can survive out there? H---, man, the straight world will eat you alive! I know, man! I tried. I was All-American. You think that was good enough? S--- no! You don't stand a chance out there, man!"

"Maybe not, but I've got to try!" Peter said softly, watching Sheik carefully, not knowing how he would react.

Apparently the fight inside had stopped. Only the low hum of music and voices now invaded their privacy. The panic in Peter was gone, replaced by fatigue. He felt so tired. He wanted Sheik to understand—not so much because he knew the man could turn the club against him as a traitor, but because he liked and respected him. But whether Sheik understood or not, Peter had made up his mind. There would be no turning back.

"Look, man. All I want to do is go to school."

"I guess I've always known," Sheik mumbled at last and sighed deeply. "I just want to know one thing, man."

"What?"

"Are you turning on us?"

"No, man!" Peter exclaimed emphatically. "I'm a Saint. I'll always be a Saint. I'm not going anywhere, man. Just to school."

For a long moment, Sheik stared hard at Peter. It was as though he were trying to measure the strength of Peter's commitment; as though he were making a hard decision.

"I envy you, man," he whispered at last in a tone Peter had never heard before. "I hope you make it."

Then he was gone. Never again would he be close enough to Peter to speak to him.

Peter smoked three more cigarettes standing alone out in front of that bar. For some reason, a part of him did not want to leave. Never before had he willingly walked away from a friend. He felt so terribly unsure of himself. Once again he found himself alone.

With great effort, he at last pushed himself off the wall and walked slowly to Sheik's bike parked at the curb. He took the cross from his neck and draped it around the handlebars where Sheik was sure to find it. Then with one last look at where he had been, Peter turned to where he was going.

PART THREE

FROM
TRASH
TO
TREASURE

Introduction

It is not often that we think of the impact we have on other people's lives. This is particularly true when we try to help and see no immediate effect. We quickly become discouraged when there is no apparent change for the better. Oftentimes we give up in dismay.

I have often wondered what would have happened to Peter if the old priest had never tried to reach out to him, or if Ed had given up on him, or if the dean of the junior college had written him off as a lost cause. Most of those people saw no immediate positive change in Peter's attitude or way of life, and yet they all persisted, each in his own way, in his own time.

At the age of twenty, Peter had stood poised on the threshold of destiny, facing the single most important decision of his life. He could choose to stay with the bikers and take his chances with the rest of them. And who would blame him? Or he could choose to leave the bikers and enter school. It was a choice only he could make. It was a choice he had to make. What he chose would determine the course of his life.

Peter chose to enter school; to take the risk of failure and rejection once more. He decided to take charge of his life and attempt to direct its course, rather than allow other people or situations to take him where they would—like a ship adrift. He chose to be a victim no longer, but to become a survivor. A survivor with purpose, with direction, with meaning for his life. It was a leap of faith far greater than any he had ever attempted—faith in himself, in other people, and in the hope that there might be a place for him somewhere out there among people who seemed to have found theirs.

Sitting here at this typewriter in a time far removed from that day so long ago, I know without a doubt that Peter would have made a different choice had it not been for the presence of the priest and Ed and the dean. Without their interest, help, and support, Peter never would have had the courage to try.

And who would have thought it would be the voice of a mother he could not even remember that would make the greatest difference? Or a song she had taught him when he was a small child? It is incredible to think a gift given twenty years earlier would make the greatest impact upon his life.

But such is the nature of childhood. It can become a time bomb ticking out its doom for an adult life. Or it can become a fertile source of nutrients, out of which a struggling adult can draw the necessities for a healthy, flourishing life.

Sometimes it is the little things that make the greatest difference. Sometimes it is the hope they offer that inspires the dream. Such was the case with Peter.

Although it would be a few years later, the time would come when Peter would build a fire and burn his colors. He would be a Saint no longer.

Twelve

Martin Luther King had been dead less than a year. Racial tensions were running high all across the country as the Black Power movement provided an ethnic model for other minorities in their quest for recognition and equality. Unlike the Native Americans who bravely and foolishly took their stand at Wounded Knee and were promptly overrun by the great-grandsons of the U.S. Cavalry, the Black Panthers and Brown Berets spread their forces in a political weave that left its indelible thread throughout the social fabric of the times. National uncertainties so stirred the American people into a frenzy of insecurity that the masses plunged headlong into minority class consciousness as a means of retaining some identity, some idea of who and what they were in a world turned senseless and meaningless by a mounting death toll in Vietnam. Young people, in particular, reflected the times in their anti-war marches, their acid-rock music, reality-distorting drugs, and recreational sex. The youth culture, mirroring the times, was a hotbed of seething passions, where ethnic consciousness was the only consciousness.

But Peter was unaware of the rival forces in conflict all around him when he started his first day as a teacher's aide in the small ghetto elementary school. As outlined by the principal, his duties were to assist the teacher in the classroom and monitor the older kids in the cafeteria and on the playground so the teachers could take their much-needed rest periods. Although he was not sure about being in a classroom under the close supervision of another adult, Peter's confidence swelled as he thought about the monitoring functions. After all, how hard could it be to watch over a bunch of youngsters?

As he stepped out on the playground that first day, he was met by a swarm of kids. They wanted to know who he was, why he was there, and what class he would be working in. His head swirling from the sudden attention, he took his time answering each question to make sure he and his answer would look "cool" in the eyes of his young admirers. He did not notice the small boy making his way slowly through the milling crowd. At last the boy stood directly in front of him, his head barely reaching Peter's waist. Totally ignored, the boy stood there for a moment grinning, then with a force greater than his small body, he reached up and hit Peter in the groin.

135

The shock of the blow forced a sharp cry from Peter's lips as he buckled under the pain. His eyes glazed with tears, he saw the little boy dart through the crowd as he headed for anonymity among the other children playing on the grounds.

Laughing and cheering, the others made a path for him and waited eagerly to see what Peter would do.

"Go, Tiny, go!" they shouted at the little boy. "Run, run, run!"

Gritting his teeth and sucking in a deep breath, Peter was after him the moment the shock began to wear off. Grimacing as he ran, it did not take too many strides to catch up with the scurrying little varmint. Catching the boy by the shoulders, Peter pulled him to a stop as the other children, still laughing and cheering, caught up with them.

"Leave me alone, you honkey!" the boy screeched.

Ignoring his screams, Peter grabbed the child by the ankles and flipped him upside down in midair, then held him so the boy's eyes were level with his.

"Why did you hit me?" Peter demanded. He stared into the eyes only an inch or two from his own.

For a fleeting moment Peter saw fear flash across those eyes, but just as quickly it was gone. In its place came an expression that, when coupled with the setting of the jaw, spelled defiance.

"Come on, man!" demanded Peter forcefully. "Why did you hit me? I haven't done anything to you. You don't even know me!"

Their faces practically touching, man and boy studied each other insolently. Anxious to see what would happen next, the throng around them was silent also. Peter glared at the boy. The boy glared back.

"Answer me, you little twerp!" Peter roared, still angry, and gave the boy a little shake that sent his body jerking wildly about. "I want to know why you hit me. How would you like to be a brand new kid in school and on your very first day somebody came up to you and hit you for no reason? And all you wanted was for everybody to like you?"

Peter had not meant to say that last. It just slipped out. Suddenly self-conscious, he began to lose his anger. But just as his own emotions were calming, Peter noticed a change in the boy he still held in front of him. The frozen features seemed to melt and the eyes became clouded with tears.

"I'm sorry," the boy whispered.

That did it. The anger was all gone now. Pulling him to his chest, Peter put the boy's feet back on the ground and hugged him tight. The boy did not resist.

"It's OK, man," Peter whispered back. "We'll just forget it this time. But don't ever do it again. OK?"

Peter learned later that Tiny was the youngest of eight children. His father had been a leader in the local Black Panther movement. In a confrontation with police, it was a white officer who had shot his father. It was a white officer who later arrested his father and took him to jail. It was a white district attorney who prosecuted his father in court. It was a white judge who heard the case. And it was an all-white jury that sent his father to prison for ten years, leaving the family to survive as best it could. The mother was in poor health and could do little to support the family. They survived on welfare. The kids were left to their own devices with little adult supervision. Like his brothers and sisters, Tiny spent most of his free time on the street.

Raising his small fist in the symbol of the Black Power movement, Tiny walked away from Peter in a strut as the crowd of onlookers dissolved. The confrontation was over and they could all go back to what they had been doing. Except for one little girl.

"You're nice," she said matter-of-factly after the other children were gone. Peter expected to see a grin accompanying those words. But there was none. Only empty, sad eyes, looking at him beneath bangs that needed to be cut.

"Yeah?" he answered her. "What makes you think so?"

"Because you didn't hit Tiny."

The girl's answer caught Peter by surprise. What a reason to think somebody was nice, he thought. Curious that she would say such a thing, he studied the girl's face for some insight. All he saw were those same sad, unchanging brown eyes and the now practically healed bruise under her left eye.

"How did you get the bruise?" he asked, pointing to his own left cheek.

Her eyes faltered for just a second.

"I fell down."

"Yeah?" Peter could tell she was lying. "Who hit you?"

"Nobody."

"Nobody who?" Peter pressed.

The girl did not answer.

"I've got to go now," she said at last, starting to move away.

"Hey, wait a minute!" Peter called after her. "What's your name?"

"Tami."

Tami was by far the prettiest and smartest girl in the school. Now a sixth-grader, she commanded the respect and admiration of every teacher. Never a discipline problem, the teachers loved her because she was a model student—attentive, cooperative, caring, involved. Her work was always on time and exceptional in accuracy and quality. If other students were having problems, she could be counted on to help them. She was an extraordinary little girl—so mature, so concerned about other people. It did not take a genius to see that her soon-to-blossom physical qualities, along with her developing intellectual capabilities, would set her head and shoulders above her peers in the years ahead.

As Peter got to know Tami, he became increasingly more concerned about her. For one thing, bruises appeared regularly on her face and arms. But far more serious in Peter's mind was the fact that he had never seen her smile. Not once. She was always so serious, as though life were a burden she could bear only with the greatest effort. Even while jumping rope or playing kickball on the playground, she did not smile or laugh. It was as though play were work she took very seriously.

One day a couple of months later, Peter left the school building long after everyone else was gone. He had stayed late to finish grading some papers for the teacher and change the bulletin board in the classroom.

As he neared his car, Peter heard boys laughing. The sound seemed to come from one of the classrooms. Curious as to why any kids would still be on the school grounds, Peter went to investigate.

A five-foot hedge surrounded the building, leaving a space about three feet wide between hedge and wall. As he followed the sound of voices, it became clear that the boys were in the space between the hedge and the building. He was not concerned so much that they were there as with what they might be doing.

"You go first," one husky male voice was saying.

"No, man, I ain't never done it before!" exclaimed another. "She's your girlfriend. You go first!"

Racing back to an opening in the hedge, Peter moved quickly along the narrow space. He slowed as he neared the corner of the building that separated him from the boys. Careful not to make a sound, he peeked around.

What he saw frightened, shocked, and angered him. Three boys were on their knees in a semicircle. One boy, who seemed the oldest, had his pants down around his knees and was holding his erect penis in his hand. Tami was lying on her back with her head resting on her schoolbooks, watching. Her dress was pulled up around her waist. Her shoes, socks, and panties were lying in the grass beside her.

Apart from the fact that a sixth-grader was involved in such a thing, what shocked Peter most was that Tami seemed to be *letting* it happen, as though she really did not mind. Having three boys looking at her body naked from the waist down did not seem to bother her, nor did she seem concerned about what they were saying or were about to do.

As always, her sad brown eyes were expressionless as though there were no feelings behind them

"What the h--- are you boys doing?" Peter barked and stepped suddenly out from the corner.

Three heads jerked around simultaneously. Then followed a scurrying as they dove under the hedge to freedom. Peter had never seen them before, but he was sure they were students from the junior high up the street. More concerned about Tami, Peter did not chase them.

"Tami! Pull your dress down!" he yelled. She was still lying on the ground, making no effort to cover herself.

Stunned by what he had stumbled upon, Peter watched Tami critically and with a great deal of concern as she slowly sat up and pulled down her dress. She did not seem embarrassed that he had discovered them or about what they were doing. She acted as though it were the most natural thing in the world, something that happened every day.

Agitated, Peter struggled to decide what to do. Since their first meeting on the playground, he had grown fond of Tami. He considered her a special friend among the other children in the school and felt a certain protectiveness because of the sadness that seemed so much a part of her life, although he had no way of knowing its source.

"Tami, don't you know what they were going to do?" he asked at last in a sudden blast of emotion.

"Yes," she answered, looking at him curiously.

"Well, why didn't you try to stop them?" he demanded, suddenly angry at her casual treatment of something so important.

"I'm a girl," she stated flatly as though that explained everything.

Speechless, Peter watched her slowly pick up her panties and stuff them into her shoes along with her socks. Then picking up the shoes and books, she walked past Peter and around the corner of the building.

"Tami! Wait a minute," Peter pleaded. "Look. Just because you are a girl does not mean you have to let boys do whatever they want. You know that, don't you?"

For a long moment the pretty girl looked at him, her expression confused as though she were trying to understand what he had said. Then, as though the data did not compute, the confusion vanished and her eyes once again became expressionless.

"I've got to go now," she stated simply.

Frustrated, he let her go. Apparently what had happened was nothing new to her. Could it be that at the age of eleven she had resigned herself to being sexually exploited? But how could that happen? Deeply troubled, Peter pondered what he should do. Should he keep it to himself and take the risk that it would happen again, or should he tell someone? But who? Her mother? Father? The school principal? How could he walk up to a child's father and tell him that he, Peter, had caught the man's daughter having sex with three boys? Who would believe him? And yet it was abundantly clear that all was not as it should be. Tami needed help. If he did not help her, who would? But how?

After long and careful thought, Peter decided the best way to help Tami was to tell her parents what he had seen. She lived only a block from the school. He parked at the curb and walked slowly up the sidewalk to the front door. It was a small house in desperate need of new paint. One of the front windows was cracked and held together by masking tape. There was an old car in the driveway.

As he approached the door, Peter could hear someone shouting inside—a man's voice, deep and harsh. He sounded angry. Or drunk. Or both. For a moment Peter hesitated. Maybe this was not a good time to talk to her parents. Maybe he should come back another time. What if they became angry at him for trying to help?

The door was opened by a frail, slender woman. Her hair was long like Tami's, and strands of it lay matted in sweat along her forehead. There was pain and fear in her eyes. The shouting had stopped.

Not sure of what was happening inside, Peter tried to explain to the anxious woman why he was there. As briefly as he could, he told her about Tami.

"O my G--!" she gasped through the screen door that separated them. "Please don't tell her father. He'd kill her! Promise me you won't tell him!" she demanded in a hoarse voice barely above a whisper.

"All right!" Peter assured her. "But what about Tami?"

"Tami?" she asked as though the thought had just come to her.

"Yes, Tami! What about her?"

"Don't worry about her," the woman said hurriedly. "She's a big girl now and can take care of herself. Besides, it's none of your business what she does, or doesn't do, for that matter! Why don't you just go away and leave us alone?"

"Who's at the d--- door?" demanded the male voice.

"Just a salesman," the woman shouted over her shoulder. The fear had returned to her eyes. "Now you go away and don't ever come back!" she instructed, and the door slammed in his face.

That was not the last time Peter would encounter parents who seemed too absorbed in their own troubles to care about those of their children. Nor was it the last time he would be told by an angry parent to mind his own business. Again and again he would be told he had no right to interfere in a family or tell them how to raise their children. Twice he was reported to the principal. Both times he was reprimanded and told to limit his work to the schoolyard and the hours of the workday.

"Most of the kids who attend this school come from broken, troubled families," the principal explained to Peter. "All of them have serious problems at home. I don't like it any more than you do. But there really is just not a whole lot we can do about it—except make things worse for the kids by butting into their home life."

142

As the days and weeks passed into months, Peter came to care more and more about the kids in the school, despite his great effort not to, and he began to seek ways to help them that would not involve visiting their homes or talking with their parents. There were Tiny and Tami. And Martha, the overweight thirteen-year-old daughter of a migrant family that had assumed a Chicano identity. Her father was an active member of the Brown Berets, the radical violent arm of the Chicano power movement. Trained and pushed to be aggressive, little provocation was needed to send Martha into a violent rage, with painful consequences for her victim.

There was Ronnie, a tall, muscular kid who was the butt of everybody's jokes. For some reason the other kids picked on him unmercifully. Often they would hit him as they passed, sometimes with blows that made him flinch. Despite his size, not once did Peter see him try to fight back. Always avoiding others' eyes, he moved listlessly about the school as though he deserved the punishment given him every day.

Then there was Paul, another son of a Black Panther family, who had a measurable IQ well above average but sat in the back of the class, making little or no effort to do the assignments. Or Jason, who smoked pot in the bathrooms and often brought drugs of various kinds on campus to sell to the other kids. And Susie, the shoplifter. Bragging to the other kids of her exploits, she kept the school supplied with chewing gum and other treats.

Then there were Katie, and Joe, and Mark, and Karen, and . . . on and on it went, a seemingly endless list of wonderful kids whom Peter came to love, but whose lives were so distorted and troubled that they already were on track for self-destruction.

To this point, their worlds had consisted of life at home, at school, and on the street, none of which was enough to ensure their survival, not to mention their success. They needed something more. Something special. They needed someone to care in a way different from the teachers—perhaps in a way that only someone who had been there could.

Thirteen

Peter's entire world was changing. In a matter of a few short months he had been transformed from an active member of Satan's Saints to just another ex-biker who continued to feel some sense of identity with the club; from making his living as a busboy to being a teachers' aide in a classroom filled with young, vulnerable lives; from living each moment for the pleasure that might be derived to preparing for a worthwhile future; and, most painful, from having the support of others like himself to having no support at all.

Like the other times when there had been sudden and dramatic moves that separated him permanently from those he cared most about, Peter found himself on his own, alone. Now considered an outsider by the bikers, they wanted little to do with him. He felt uncomfortable in their presence, as though he no longer fit. Buck, his closest companion in the club, was dead. Michael was dead. Ed was gone, buried somewhere deep in the Canadian wilderness. Susan was married and raising a family. And his brothers were both in the military.

Pleased with the other developments in his life, Peter became acutely aware of just how alone he really was on the evening he talked with Tami's mother and was told to mind his own business. He knew what was happening to the girl was not right and would eventually hurt her badly. But those who were supposed to care most about her did not seem to care at all. Deeply concerned, Peter felt he had to do something to help her. But what he had thought was the best thing had turned out to be a mistake. He could not afford mistakes. Not when it involved the lives of kids.

Frantically searching his own mind for an answer, Peter felt overwhelmed by his own inadequacy and, for the first time he could remember, decided he needed help. He needed somone to talk to, to tell about Tami and the other kids, someone who could tell him what to do. At that moment he felt his aloneness most intensely. Everyone he trusted enough to turn to for help was gone.

Almost everyone. There was still one person—Father Paul. Yes, Father Paul would know what to do! Some of Peter's tension and anxiety began to dissipate as the thought of turning to the old priest blossomed in his mind. Relieved, he soon relaxed and slipped into a fitful, dream-filled sleep.

This dream was so clear it seemed to last forever. His mother and sister were there, calling to him, beckoning him. He could see their faces—they looked just as they had the last time he saw them—more than ten years before. But he was separated from them by a bottomless pit filled with a raging current that would sweep him away, should he fall in. And yet he would die if he remained where he was! Somehow he had to get across. Only there in his mother's arms would he be safe. Several times he ventured out into the space, clinging desperately to rocks that suddenly appeared, each time getting almost within arm's reach, when the chasm would widen and the rocks would vanish, leaving him to fight frantically to reclaim his place on the other side. It seemed if he could ever do it right—whatever "it" was—he would be able to cross the gaping chasm. It was only his inadequacy that kept him from his mother and sister. Frustrated and angry, Peter tried again and again to bridge the gulf, only to panic at the last minute as the gap widened and the rocks disappeared.

Mercifully the dream ended with the ring of an alarm clock in the apartment next door. Although Peter did not know it at the time, similar nightmares would occur at irregular intervals during the following years, ending only when he launched his search for his lost family.

Although it was still early, Peter showered and dressed hurriedly. He was anxious to follow up on his resolution of the night before.

The priest was celebrating early Eucharist alone in the chapel. Peter entered and took a seat at the rear of the room. If Father Paul had heard someone come in, he gave no sign.

At last the candles on the altar were extinguished and the service was over. Peter stood up and moved hesitantly down the aisle.

"Father Paul?" He spoke softly as he neared the priest.

"Hello, Peter!" The old man greeted him with a warm smile. "I've been expecting you."

"You've been expecting me?" Peter was confused. How could the man possibly have known he would be coming, when Peter himself did not know until last night?

"To return," the priest explained, his face aglow with welcome.

"What made you think I would return?" Peter asked a little defensively. It made him uneasy to think he had become predictable. One of the keys to survival was to keep your opponent guessing.

The priest placed his hand on Peter's shoulder and they walked slowly toward the rear of the chapel.

"Because there is no greater power in all the world than God's love. It is an irresistible force in the life of one who has known its presence even once. In it, all things are possible. Even you!"

"And you think it is this irresistible force that has brought me here this morning?"

"Just as surely as a child, lost and alone, yearns for the comfort of a father's arms!" The priest smiled again, his eyes dancing with a knowledge that left Peter feeling terribly unsure of himself. Watching closely as Peter tried to understand what he had said, the priest laughed warmly and patted his shoulder.

"Oh Peter, Peter. How long will you continue to resist the will of God in your life?"

Peter did not answer. Such talk made him feel frightened and vulnerable. How could he ever again trust another person after surviving the ultimate betrayal of his parents? It was only by taking full control of his own life that he had survived. And yet, what about that time on the beach after he had been kicked out of his adopted home? For two weeks he had tried to help himself, but could do nothing. Was it not God who had delivered him from his own helplessness then? Threatened by the thought, Peter forcibly pushed it away. "I didn't come here to talk to God!" he snapped. "I came to talk to you."

"That'll do for now," the priest said, still smiling. "Come have a bite of breakfast with me and we will listen."

They walked across the street to a small restaurant that was serving breakfast. After they had ordered, the priest turned again to Peter.

"Now, tell us what is troubling you."

The "we" and the "us" were a little unnerving, but Peter plunged ahead anyway. For ten minutes he talked without interruption. The thoughts, feelings, and concerns poured out in a rush of words and frustrated gestures. Spent at last, he sighed and sat back in his chair.

"I just don't know what to do," he concluded.

"You really care about those kids, don't you?"

The question caught Peter by surprise. He had not thought about whether he cared. He had learned early in life that to care too much about another human being brought only pain and suffering, for sooner or later that person would be gone from his life never to return. He had decided it was better—and safer—not to care. It frightened him to think that he might.

"A little, maybe," he answered at last.

"That's good, my son. Some of the best healing comes from touching another's wound."

"H---, man! I don't want to heal anybody. I just want to help Tami and those other kids!" Peter exclaimed, not understanding what the priest meant. "They didn't do anything to deserve the kind of lives they live. They deserve so much better. All I want is for them to have a chance!"

Tears began to well up in his eyes as he struggled to make the priest understand. Peter could not bear the thought of other children having to go through a childhood as devastating as his had been—a childhood that robbed them of the joy of being alive, of discovering life with its infinite possibilities.

Huddled together over steaming cups of coffee, the two men talked long into the morning, discussing one option after another as a means for improving the quality of life for the kids at the school. After all their ideas had been scrutinized in detail, and most discarded for one reason or another, they came to the conclusion that the best way for Peter to help the kids was to teach them to help themselves. In the long run, there was not a person or institution that these kids, or most of them, could really count on to protect and care for them. They would have to take care of themselves if they were going to survive. Even more important, if they wanted to do more than merely survive, they would have to make their own breaks.

They further agreed that the best way to hold the kids' attention long enough to make a difference was through some kind of competition. That was something they all could understand. Recognizing that not all forms of competition were healthy, the next decision concerned the form this competition would take. The answer was clear and simple. Athletics. The best way for Peter to help the kids help themselves was through an athletic program that required enough physical and emotional commitment to allow teaching in the areas of physical and mental health.

As the idea began to crystallize in his mind, Peter became excited. For the first time, he sensed that perhaps there could be a purpose in his life, something to live and work for beyond mere survival. To have a reason to exist and a direction was new and very exciting. It felt good! It felt great! He could not wait to get started.

Peter did not know then, or for several years to come, that he had taken the first step toward freeing himself from the prison of his childhood. He had made the suffering of others more important than his own and had vowed to do something about it. He had begun to reach out in a purposeful and meaningful attempt to improve the life of somone else. Until now, his effort and attention had always been turned inward, in a concentrated attempt to survive each day as he struggled to reach adulthood and independence.

Reversing the flow of life-giving energy to include other people was one of the most significant changes to occur in Peter's life. At some level of consciousness, it was a statement to himself and to the world that he no longer felt his personal survival was threatened on a daily basis. He had become comfortable enough in his own existence to be able to afford caring about other people, and he felt confident enough to take the risk that caring required. It was an emotional turning point.

"I'm so glad I came to talk to you!" Peter smiled at the old priest across the table. He was amazed how comfortable he felt with the man. "I really didn't know what to do."

"Well, I'm glad you came, too, Peter," the priest smiled back. "There are two rules of thumb I use whenever I find myself trying to figure out what to do. Particularly when it comes to other people and their lives. Do you want to know what they are?"

"Sure," Peter answered eagerly, anxious to learn.

"The first is this: When you find yourself in a situation where you do not know what to do, do nothing. Take your time. Be patient. Listen for God's direction in the midst of quiet stillness. It is better to do nothing than to rush in and do something that in the long run does more harm than good. First, do no harm. Then, try to determine what love requires of you."

"I don't understand."

"Jesus told us to love one another as he has loved us. He also said that the greatest of all the commandments was to love God and one's neighbor as oneself. The challenge to all Christians is to determine what love requires of them in every situation."

"But how do you find out what love requires in every situation?" What the priest was saying was beginning to make sense and Peter knew it was important.

"It's really not so hard." The priest smiled warmly. "Simply ask yourself a question. And this is my second rule of thumb: Ask yourself, What would Jesus do? There are not many situations in which the answer to that question will not be pretty clear."

The simplicity of the answer left Peter stunned. What would Jesus do? For years Peter had sought a model for living and some way of knowing what was right and wrong, apart from his instincts. Maybe this is what the priest meant when he had said, "Jesus is the way."

As time went on, Peter came to realize more and more the importance of that simple question. It became the unspoken basis for all he did. Despite the countless situations in which what Jesus would obviously do or say differed dramatically from what Peter wanted to do, and was therefore ignored, that queston became the moral and ethical standard in his life. It was the yardstick by which he came to measure all his thoughts and actions.

"One more thing," warned the priest as he held out his hand. "When you offer your hand to another in love and caring, expect to have a nail driven through it from time to time."

Leaving Father Paul with a promise to attend church the following morning, Peter drove straight to the beach to begin making plans for the athletic program. He had so much to think about! And all of it was important. He parked along the beach and walked to the long finger of rocks projecting out into the surf. At the very end of the jetty, once again, as in countless times past, he claimed his special place in the midst of sand, sea, and sky.

He had been there hardly five minutes when he heard a voice behind him.

"Hi!"

Peter turned quickly. It was the girl he had met the last time he was here! She was wearing cut-offs and a halter and was even more beautiful than he remembered. With heart and mind racing, he at last found his voice.

"Hi!"

"I thought that was you!" She stepped gingerly among the rocks to join him. "I saw you as you walked across the beach. Do you mind if I join you?"

"No! No, sit down," Peter exclaimed. He had been sure he would never see her again. Yet here she was! Even more amazing, she actually seemed glad to see him again.

Peter learned her name was Wendy, and they had graduated from the same high school. She was only two years behind him, and he wondered why he had not seen her around campus. He also discovered they were attending the same junior college. Most of her classes were during the day rather than at night. She planned to graduate with sixty semester hours and transfer to a college in another state. Peter listened intently to her every word, wanting to learn as much about her as possible.

"And so, what brings you out here all alone?" she asked at last.

That was all the invitation Peter needed. He spent the next hour telling her about his job at the school, the kids, how he worried about them, and finally, about his talk with the priest. Occasionally she would ask questions.

"You must be a very special person to care about those kids that much," she said when he was finished. Her deep brown eyes spoke a respect for him that he had never seen before. He was more used to eyes filled with contempt.

"Who, me?" he laughed. "You must be kidding! There's nothing special about me. I'm a nobody. But a nobody who cares!" he was surprised to hear himself say.

"That's what makes you so special!"

At that moment, Peter felt special. Not because of what she said, but because she was there with him. Obviously a girl of class, attractive enough to have many boyfriends, and certainly intelligent enough to know what she wanted, she chose to be there with him when she could be doing a thousand other things. He did not want her to leave. He wanted those soft, caring eyes to look at him forever.

Not sure what was happening to him, Peter spent the entire afternoon with Wendy. The time passed unnoticed until at last the sun began touching the distant horizon. Uncertain of almost every aspect of his life until then, there were two things about which he had no doubt as he watched her car disappear in the distance—he would see her again Friday, and he was in love with her.

Fourteen

Dr. Campbell, the principal, listened patiently as Peter explained the proposed athletic program. He was interested in anything that would benefit his school's children and faculty.

"That all sounds very good, Peter." He casually lit his pipe. "Heaven knows these kids need something to do in their free time besides roaming the streets. Have you given any thought to how the program is to be financed?"

Peter knew this was a critical issue. Somehow he had to convince the principal he could raise the money. Asking the school system to sponsor an athletic program was out of the question.

"I'm not sure exactly how much money is involved," he answered.

"Well, let's see. You will have to hire a coach and someone to run the program."

"I'll coach and run the program," Peter interjected, barely able to keep the excitement out of his voice.

"I can't pay you more than you're already getting, Peter."

"I know."

"You would have to start from scratch and organize a league. That will take time and a lot of work."

"Yes, I know," Peter repeated, still undaunted.

"What about officials and referees?"

"We can get male teachers to do that. I'm sure Mr. Smith will ref our home games if we ask him," Peter said.

"Yes, I think he would," Dr. Campbell mused. "There is still equipment and insurance. We must have insurance."

"Yes, I've thought about that, too," Peter answered. "The kids and I could do fund-raisers. I'm sure we could raise enough money to pay for some equipment and the insurance."

The prinicpal eyed Peter through a film of pipe smoke as he thought over the details of the proposal. Peter watched him closely as though attempting to read his thoughts. It was the tightening of the muscles around the eyes and jaw that told Peter the proposal was about to be turned down. Now, while the decision still hung in the balance, was the time to play his ace!

"I thought we could do a weekly grade and conduct check on each of the players, with the stipulation that failure would result in ineligibility to play in that week's game." Peter saw the light of renewed interest come on in the principal's eyes.

Dr. Campbell sat forward in his chair. "A grade and conduct check?"

"Yes, sir. We could set a standard for eligibility. Those not achieving the standard would have to sit out a week," Peter explained. "If I know these kids, they would do anything to be able to play—even make good grades and behave!"

He liked the idea! Peter knew then he would get his chance. Dr. Campbell would approve anything that would inspire his children to perform academically and also ease some of the volatile tensions in the school.

"You have a good idea here, Peter," he concluded after a moment. "I will have to clear it through the superintendent, of course. In the meantime, you contact other schools to see if they are interested in participating and give me some written plans on how you intend to raise the necessary funds."

Keeping his emotions firmly in control, Peter stood to leave. "I'll get back to you as soon as I have them," he said, shaking the man's hand.

"By the way, I didn't even ask. What sports are we talking about?"

"Boys' football and baseball. Girls' cheerleading and softball," Peter answered with a grin that gave away his excitement.

Once outside the principal's office, he could hold back no longer. Dancing merrily down the hall, he roared out a cheer. Several heads popped out of classroom doors to scowl their disapproval. But nothing could subdue the ex-biker at that moment. He had found a way to help his kids! He had never been more excited, or more determined.

It took no more than a week to set up a game schedule involving ten other schools. They were all interested. The fact that none of the others was a ghetto school and they all were three, four, even five times as large did not bother Peter. What bothered him was that he had just five weeks to field and prepare a team. The first game was only a little over a month away and would be played at home, in front of the entire school and any parents who could attend. He still had to get the equipment and money for the insurance. And teach the boys to play football. And how in the world was he going to teach girls to be cheerleaders? Fighting the panic that comes from feeling overwhelmed, Peter knew he needed a few miracles.

The first one came the day he presented his written plans to Dr. Campbell. He was trying desperately to appear confident and convince the man all was under control.

"Well, Peter, this looks very good," Dr. Campbell commented after glancing over the typewritten two-page report. "You have lined up some pretty stiff competition. You realize these other schools are a lot bigger and have more students to draw from, don't you?" He looked at Peter over his glasses.

"Yes, sir, I know that."

"Do you really think we can beat a few of them?" he asked, obviously doubtful.

"We can beat them all!" Peter exclaimed confidently.

"You see, sir, we have something they don't have. Most of our kids are losers. At school, at home, on the street, everywhere. Compared to other kids, ours really don't have much to feel proud of themselves about." Peter paused a moment as though weighing his next words. "You ever been a loser, Dr. Campbell?"

"Not in the sense you mean," he answered.

"Well, I have. And I've lived with losers. Get a bunch of losers together, give them a common challenge and a *reason* for winning—a real reason—and watch what happens. I can almost guarantee you, these kids are going to win. You watch!"

The principal smiled warmly, despite the doubt that still lingered in his eyes.

"Well, let's hope so," he stated. "Now I've got some good news for you. The superintendent has approved our plans. Also, since you are volunteering your time, he thinks the school district can find the money to pay the insurance."

"That's great!" Peter exclaimed. Not having to raise the insurance money would help a great deal.

"That's not all!" Dr. Campbell continued. "Now, this is a long shot, but it's worth a try. I know the owner of a sports store here in town. Here are his name and phone number." He handed Peter a piece of paper. "Why don't you give him a call and go see him. Tell him what you are trying to do and why. Who knows? Maybe he would be interested in sponsoring the team."

Peter wasted no time getting in touch with the owner of the sporting-goods store. He had an appointment that very afternoon.

Mr. Holtzheimer had immigrated to the United States from Warsaw after the war. Starting with nothing, he had built a chain of stores and now dominated the market in that region of the state. He was a tough-minded businessman, firm and to the point.

Peter began by trying to tell the busy man his plans for the athletic program. But he was cut short before he could finish.

"What do you want from me?" the man asked, looking directly into Peter's eyes. "You want me to supply some equipment, yes?"

His directness caught Peter off guard. Although he did not want to ask too much, for fear of getting nothing, the man was demanding an answer.

"Well, sir . . . uh . . ."

"How much can you pay?" the man cut him short again.

"We don't have any money." Peter at last found his voice. "The kids will have to raise it somehow."

"How?" the man pressed on.

"Well, we're not real sure yet. Car washes, I guess. And candy sales, maybe."

"What sport?"

"Football and cheerleading."

"Cheerleading?" His eyebrows shot up.

"Yes, sir. For the girls. They need to be involved, too," Peter explained. "You see, sir, these kids . . ."

"What kids?" Again the man's question cut Peter short.

"Ghetto kids. From Avenue school."

"Ghetto? I know ghetto," the man said softly, and suddenly his eyes changed. Peter could see pain and sadness in them. For a long time the man was silent, as though remembering something long ago. Peter watched the rapidly changing expressons on the man's face. He seemed lost in another time, another place. At last Peter decided to break the silence.

"Dr. Campbell suggested that . . . "

"Dr. Campbell?" Mr. Holtzheimer looked up. "Yes, I know Dr. Campbell. He is a friend of mine. He sent you, yes?"

"Yes, sir. He thought I should talk to you and . . . " Again Peter tried to explain why he was there.

"I'll let you know," Mr. Holtzheimer stated firmly and stood up.

Hesitantly, as though not finished, Peter shook his hand. Stunned by the man's abruptness, he shrank under a feeling of defeat as he walked out. He had blown it! Somehow he had not made the man understand how important this athletic program was and how much he could help. Frustrated and depressed, he fought the urge to barge back into the man's office and try again. Instead, he went for a walk on the beach.

The following afternoon, a call came over the intercom as Peter was assisting the teacher with a math assignment.

"Peter? Can you come to the office for a minute, please?" the school secretary's voice called out.

Overcoming his surprise, Peter headed for the office, not knowing what to expect. Had another parent complained? Another reprimand from the principal was all he needed to make his day a total ruin.

A man dressed in coveralls, smoking a cigarette and holding a clipboard, was standing in the office. He looked out of place and a little uncomfortable under the watchful eye of the school secretary.

"This gentleman needs to see you," Mrs. Parks announced.

"Are you the coach?" the man asked eagerly, apparently in a hurry to be on his way. Peter smiled. It was the first time he had been called *Coach*. He had been called many things, but never that. It felt good.

"That's right," he answered. "What can I do for you?"

"Sign here." The man thrust the clipboard at him.

"What is it?" Peter asked absentmindedly. His heart leaped as he suddenly became aware of what he was holding. Tears dimmed his eyes as he tried to read. It was a delivery order from the sporting-goods store. Four new footballs and enough used football gear to equip the entire team! Peter was ecstatic! He could hardly stand still long enough to sign the order. It was the second miracle in as many days. Across the page, written in bright red letters, was "No Charge."

There was a note attached, a small piece of unlined paper folded three times. Opening it, Peter found a message scribbled in the owner's own hand: "Teach them to laugh."

Filled with gratitude, he helped the delivery man unload the equipment.

By three o'clock that same afternoon, word had spread throughout the school. Every boy in the two upper grades had signed up to play on the team, and over half the girls wanted to be cheerleaders.

Peter felt wonderful! Already he had a schedule of ten games, the necessary insurance, a team, and now he had the equipment to begin practice. What more could he ask?

Peter stayed long after school hours were over, sorting through the equipment. Along with the footballs, there were helmets, shoulder and hip pads, practice jerseys and pants. Everything was there. Several times he caught himself daydreaming as he sat in the middle of equipment piled all around him on the floor. Across the screen of his mind flashed an endless array of dreams for his kids. Each of them was a hero, performing magnificently in front of a crowd of admiring and cheering fans. How proud their parents would be! And the kids! Each of them would feel really special!

Suddenly Peter was crying. Sitting alone in that big empty room, the child in him once again cried out its need to be loved and accepted. What he would have given to have someone proud of him! For what seemed a lifetime, he fought to control his feelings. But the sobs kept coming. Again and again they doubled him over in spasms of grief until at last the pain subsided.

Exhausted, Peter must have dozed. He was shocked to find the sun setting. Glancing at his watch, he saw it was already past six. He was supposed to pick Wendy up at a quarter to seven! He dashed to his car and home to get cleaned up. Not taking time to shower, he pulled up at Wendy's house only a couple of minutes late.

It took all the courage Peter could muster to drag himself out of the security of the car and up the sidewalk to the front door. The house was ablaze with lights. He was kept from bolting only by his desperate desire to see Wendy again and the fact that she was expecting him. Taking a deep breath and holding it a long second, he determinedly reached out and pushed the doorbell.

A moment later the front door opened and Peter was face to face with Wendy's father. Hard, measuring eyes probed his before a smile appeared on the tanned face and the screen door opened. Extending his hand, the man clasped Peter's in a grip like a vise and pulled him into the house.

"Come on in here!" he exclaimed as Peter followed the pull on his arm. "You must be Peter."

"Y . . . yes, sir!" Peter stammered, overcome with self-consciousness. This was the first real date he had ever had, and the first time he had ever met a girl's father. He did not know what to do or say. He felt out of place, as though he did not belong there. "Is Wendy ready?"

"Almost. Come on in and meet the family," the man said and escorted him into the dining room, where the family was still seated around the table. "This is my wife, Jane, and Wendy's two sisters." He indicated the women at the table. "She has two brothers, too, but they are both in the service."

After greetings all around, Peter was made to sit in the chair apparently vacated by Wendy when she had left to finish getting ready.

He could barely lift his eyes from his lap. He knew they were all looking at him. Desperately, he wanted them to like him because he liked Wendy so much. But deep inside, he knew they would not. What would they think if they knew he was an ex-biker? Or that he was so bad his adopted parents had kicked him out? Or that not even his own parents loved him enough to keep him? These and a thousand similar thoughts bombarded Peter as he sat in front of Wendy's family, trying desperately not to let his feelings show. The longer he sat, the more convinced he became that if they ever found out what he was really like, they would reject him on the spot.

Trying to remember his very best manners, he fielded their questions as best he could. Just at the point when he could stand it no longer and was edging forward on the chair to be in a better position to bolt out the front door, Wendy came into the room. She must have seen the panic in his eyes, because she did not break stride as she took his hand and pulled him up from the chair and toward the door.

"We've got to hurry or we'll be late!" she exclaimed to her family as she headed toward the door.

"Hey! Wait a minute," her father demanded, following them. "Where are you going and when can we expect you home?"

"We're going to a movie and maybe stop for a Coke somewhere afterward, Daddy," Wendy answered for Peter. "I'll be in by one. OK?"

"Well, you kids drive careful now," he warned from the front porch as he watched them get into the car. In the rear-view mirror, Peter could see him still standing on the porch as the car pulled around the corner.

"I'm so glad to see you!" he sighed when they were alone at last. She snuggled over next to him. An intoxication filled his head to feel her so close. It felt good. And frightening. He could not help remembering Susan. He had allowed himself to get close to her, too, only to have her gone from his life like all the others. Dare he try again?

Fifteen

Peter formally presented his plans for the athletic program at a faculty meeting the following Monday. He explained that the games would be held every Friday for ten weeks; they would start at one o'clock in order to be sure of being completed by the end of the school day. When a couple of teachers voiced their opposition to taking two hours of school time for the games, several others pointed out how little was accomplished academically on Friday afternoon anyway, due to the children's restless anticipation of the weekend. Closing out the school week with a game would send the children into the weekend excited and proud to be part of that school, give them something to talk about, and another reason for returning to class the following Monday.

After explaining the eligibility check, which would be conducted every Friday morning before a game, and which would include a passing grade in attitude, conduct, and academic performance from the child's teachers, the plan was enthusiastically accepted. Anything that would help prevent truancy, diminish racial tension and fighting, and improve academic performance was worth a try.

Practice began the following day after school. Peter explained the rules as he studied the expectant faces of the children sitting in a semicircle around him on the grass. Despite their obvious eagerness to be up and knocking one another down, the kids listened intently. They had already learned he meant business. The last thing any of them wanted was to do something that would get them sidelined from a game. They wanted to play!

There were approximately thirty boys out for the team and half as many girls for the cheerleading squad. It was a motley crew, to say the least, with most of the kids either overweight or undersized for their age because of poor nutrition. But already Peter felt a sense of pride. They were his kids!

First he explained what he expected of them. They were to call him Coach and nothing else—particularly not some of the less-than-respectful superlatives students sometimes used when referring to teachers or adults. They were to attend every practice unless sick and to do their best at all times. Most especially, they were to obey him. Failure in this regard could result in having to run laps, do push-ups, or miss a game. Then Peter explained the other infractions that would result in missing a game.

"If you are caught fighting on campus, or even after school in your neighborhood, I promise that you will miss that week's game. There are other ways to solve personal problems. If you are going to play ball for me and this school, then you will learn what those other ways are. Any questions?"

"Yeah, Coach, I've got a question," said Jason. "What if a nigger jumps me on my way home from school? Don't I have the right to fight back? My dad said I do. He told me he would whip me if I didn't whip the kid!"

There was an immediate reaction from the black students. Almost as one, they were on their knees, shouting.

"Who the h--- you callin' nigger, you honkey piece of white trash?"

It took two minutes and four laps around the field to get the kids calmed down. Even then the lines between black, white, and brown were clearly drawn as they clustered around Peter in their groups. Even the girls kept themselves segregated.

"All of you hear me and hear me good!" spoke Peter emphatically as the kids settled around him on the ground again. "On this team there is no black or white or brown. There is only Mike, Bobby, Paul, Tami, Susie, Jack. Just people. It does not matter to me whether you are black, white, brown, blue, green, or purple. As far as I am concerned, we are all in this thing together, like brothers and sisters, a big family. We are going to practice together, learn together, eat together, play together, and win together. Is that clear? Name calling is like fighting. It will not be tolerated! If you do it, you will miss a game. That's a promise! Do you all understand me?"

There was a rapid nodding of heads. They understood. They did not like it, but they understood. Or maybe he mistook their relief for displeasure.

"Now," Peter continued, "there are several other ways you can miss a game. One is by not doing and turning in your homework. You have to get at least a C average in all your subjects each week in order to play in that week's game. If you are having trouble in one of your classes and cannot find anyone to help you, come see me. I'll help you.

"Another way is by getting in trouble with a teacher—like disobeying, talking back, or disrupting the class. Get the

162

idea? Another is cutting class. One unexcused absence and you will sit out that week's game. You want to play ball, you come to class. Every day.

"Now, getting in trouble with the law is another way you can miss a game. Like stealing hubcaps, or shoplifting, or smoking pot, or doing drugs. In fact, you do any of these things, and you will miss more than one game! Do you all understand me? And one more thing. There will be no messing around with the opposite sex. You will keep your hands and other body parts to yourself!"

Every eye suddenly found something else to look at. Most of the kids were embarrassed at the mention of sex. Others were suddenly self-conscious. Peter could tell the difference. How he wished they were all just embarrassed!

"Do you all understand?" he asked finally. "Any questions?" They all understood and there were no questions. He did not think there would be.

For the next few weeks practice was held every day after school, from three-thirty until six o'clock. Peter was pleased and impressed by how hard they all worked. Their commitment and determination made him want to work harder to give them the very best he had to offer.

The kids seemed to be thriving under the new system of discipline. Slowly, as each day passed and the rules were enforced, a change began to occur both on and off campus. It soon became a major topic of conversation among the teachers over lunch. The fighting had all but stopped. When there was a flare-up, teammates would often break it up before a teacher could respond. Slowly the air in the bathrooms cleared of cigarette smoke and the odor of marijuana. Absenteeism among the upper grades was all but eliminated, and grades began to rise. But most noticeable of all seemed to be the easing of racial tension.

Having instituted a football team and cheerleader training table in the cafeteria, they all were expected to sit together at lunch. Peter was pleased to see the lines of segregation beginning to break down. Eventually it became an honor to sit at that table. Those who did not were envious. Those who did were proud and did not hesitate to show it.

Still unsure of himself and fighting contantly against his own sense of personal inadequacy, which almost daily tempted him to abort his work at the school for fear of failure, Peter thrilled to the enthusiastic encouragement of the other teachers. It was a strange and exciting feeling for other adults to actually like what he was doing rather than criticize or reject his efforts. But the pride that was trying to take root was thwarted by that ever-present sense of foreboding, that haunting sense of the disaster that waited just around the corner, should they ever find out what he was really like. It was as though there were two of him. There was Peter the coach. That Peter was OK. But Peter the person was not. The praise he received for his work was not really for him—it was for that other person, the person who seemed to be doing a good job, the person who seemed to be what they all wanted him to be.

The same was true in his relationship with Wendy. After that first date, hardly a day passed that they did not see each other or at least talk on the phone. They spent a great deal of time talking, walking on the beach, even studying together. Eventually they each acknowledged their growing romance and, as they became more emotionally intimate, began to risk physical intimacy.

Although frightened and insecure in her presence, Peter loved the time they spent together and could not seem to get enough of it. It had been a long time since he was last held by a woman. It felt good and was so desperately needed, but at the same time, it terrorized him. There was the nagging belief that she would leave him if she ever discovered who he really was.

It was this that finally drove him to propose. Despite his fears and anxiety, he needed her and did not want to risk losing her. Somehow he had to make the relationship permanent before she found out how unlovable he really was. She would not want him then. But if they were already married, maybe she would not leave.

It was a Friday evening. After Peter's class, they met at the student center, had a Coke, and talked. After driving her home, Peter parked in front of her house. For a long time they sat there talking softly and experiencing the warmth of each other's company. Peter was sure he loved her, although he was equally sure he had no idea what real love was. But he needed her and wanted her and could not bear the thought of ever losing her. Was that not love? She seemed to want and need him too. Although he could not imagine how she could possibly love him, she must feel something for him or she would not be there, he reasoned. Neither of them wanted to say good-night and go their separate ways.

Suddenly the front door of the house opened and a streak of light split the night down the length of the sidewalk. Her father's figure appeared silhouetted in the doorway.

"Come in the house, Wendy!" he barked.

"Be there in a minute," she called back cheerfully. The figure disappeared and the light was suddenly gone. Darkness enveloped them once again.

Leaning toward him, Wendy put her arms around his neck and kissed him long and passionately. Somewhere in the midst of that kiss, Peter found the words and courage he sought.

It's now or never, he thought. You love her and she loves you. You can't ask for anything more. Besides, you will never again find anyone who might want you!

"Will you marry me?" he asked tentatively.

Peter felt her body grow suddenly tense in his arms and just as suddenly relax.

"Yes," she whispered, and kissed him more passionately than before.

The front door of the house again burst open. This time her father stormed halfway down the sidewalk.

"Wendy! Come in the house now!" he demanded, making no move to leave without her.

"We need to tell our parents. Can you come to dinner Sunday night?" she asked and opened the car door to show her impatient father she was on her way.

Peter nodded.

"Is it all right for Peter to come to dinner Sunday night, Daddy?" she called to her father, still standing on the sidewalk.

"Well, yes . . . yes, I guess that would be all right," he stammered. "But you'll have to ask your mother."

"Great!" she called as she stepped out of the car. "See you Sunday night then." She blew Peter a kiss over her shoulder and followed her father into the house.

Suddenly Peter was alone. The realization of what had just occurred hit him like a blow. He had asked Wendy to marry him, to become his wife! And she had accepted!

Peter was overwhelmed with joy and an incredible fear. In a frenzy, feeling totally out of control, he drove about town for what seemed like hours. His thoughts blurred with tumultuous feelings until at last his panic drove him into full flight. Stopping only for booze, he drove up the coast—away from Wendy, the school, the kids, the team, his classes— away from the fear of exposure and failure. At last, a couple of hundred miles away, he checked into a motel for the night.

Once in the room, Peter became so drunk all feelings and thoughts were drowned in a sodden stupor, until at last he passed into a much-welcomed sleep. He spent the next two days in bed, getting up only to use the bathroom. He was buried deep within one of the gloomiest fits of depression he had ever experienced. It was like a weight on his mind and body so heavy that normal functioning was out of the question. Every ounce of energy and concentration was needed just to keep him from going berserk. How close Peter came to losing his mind that weekend, no one will ever know. It was one of the most critical tests of his will to survive he had ever faced. Although he would be plagued with periodic depression for the next ten years, never again would the stakes be so high or the danger so real.

By Sunday morning he was desperately searching for something concrete and real to hold on to—something he could trust, something that would not change or betray him. He dared not trust his own senses, thoughts, or feelings—they were a quicksand of panic, confusion, doubt, and uncertainty. Surrender to them would mean sure suffocation.

Casting about desperately, Peter became aware of just how unreal everything actually is. People, places, things—everything is uncertain—here today, gone tomorrow; friend today, foe tomorrow. Like time, everything is changing, never remaining the same. How is it possible to remain constant and unchanged amidst such change and uncertainty? How is it possible to remain sane in the midst of such insanity?

As his mind began drawing into itself, a voice pierced the chaos, soft and gentle. It was a woman's voice, singing, barely above a whisper but as clear as though it were shouting in his ear. A song Peter had learned as a child in his mother's arms. A song he had heard at other desperate times. A song that calmed his panic and quelled the madness.

"Jesus loves me, this I know, for the Bible tells me so . . ."

Suddenly Peter was a child again, watching his mother's loving face only inches from his own as she sang those words over and over. And then he was with Bo, holding his beloved dog tight against his tear-streaked cheek as they watched the panorama of another sunrise, clinging together for warmth and love. Holding onto those memories and singing that song over and over to himself, Peter cried out his fear and panic. Nauseated by its force, he let it come. All resistance was gone. He had only strength enough to hold onto the memories and the words of the song.

At long last the panic subsided. Peter's mind was clear again. He could think without fear of losing control. Breathing deeply, he washed his face and combed his hair. He left a note on the bed asking the management to bill him for use of the room. Then he drove slowly back home.

It was late afternoon when he arrived at his apartment. Wendy pulled into the parking lot just behind him.

"Peter, Peter!" she called out to him. "Where have you been? I've been worried sick about you. I tried to call a hundred times but there was never any answer. And when you didn't come by yesterday, I really got worried!"

"I'm sorry," he spoke reassuringly to her. "I didn't mean to worry you. I guess I just had to get away for a while. To think."

"Well, thank G-- you're back!" she exclaimed in relief. "Let's get you ready. You're coming to dinner tonight, remember?" A wide smile spread across her face. "You are still coming, aren't you?"

Where only hours ago had been panic and confusion, now was an incredibly soothing calm. Somewhere in all that madness, he had found some peace. It felt good to be with Wendy again. He could feel her love for him. And he sensed his love reaching out to her. The confusion in his mind was gone. He knew what he had to do. No matter how frightening, no matter how much he doubted himself, no matter how painful it might turn out to be or how much risk was involved, he had to try. He had to try to open up and love her and give her a chance to love him. He had to!

How he would have liked to just curl up in her arms and sleep for a hundred years. He felt absolutely exhausted. But not wanting to disappoint her, he hurried to get ready. After all, they were going to announce their engagement tonight, and he wanted to be at his best so she would be proud of him.

Dinner went well enough. Although Peter still felt awkward in social situations, he managed to complete the meal without a major catastrophe and was able to make small talk with Wendy's father, who was a teacher and a former coach. He believed strongly in the value of athletic programs in schools, particularly in a ghetto situation.

Peter sighed gratefully when everyone was finally finished and they retired to the living room. Peter sat down near the front door, facing the long couch on the opposite side of the room. It was there Wendy's parents settled themselves. Wendy followed Peter and claimed a seat on the arm of his chair. It was comforting to have her so near. Her sisters took other seats in the room.

Despite his unspoken belief that her family would disapprove of their marriage, Peter felt strangely calm as he sat waiting for Wendy to make the announcement. He was sure now of what he had to do, and as long as Wendy was willing, he was going to do it. It was important to have her parents' blessing, but in his mind the decision had already been made and did not rest with them.

Wendy began to speak, a little self-consciously, after everyone was finally settled. "Mother and Daddy, Peter and I have something we would like to tell you."

Maybe it was the tone of her voice more than what she had said that caused all eyes to rivet on the pair. Peter found himself looking at Wendy.

"Oh?" intoned her father at last. "And what might that be, Miss Priss?"

"Peter and I have decided to be married!" Wendy blurted out with a girlish giggle. "We want to ask for your blessing."

The announcement hung in the air for a long moment before it met with any response. Was it disappointment he saw register in her parents' eyes? Had they hoped their oldest daughter would do better? Peter caught himself intently searching each face for some sign of acceptance and approval and forced himself to relax.

"Your mother and I had hoped you would finish college before you got married," her father responded at last. "Have you thought about that?"

"Yes, Daddy. Peter and I can finish school together," she answered. "We both want degrees."

"I see." His eyes moved from the floor in front of him to Peter and back again. "Well, have you decided on a date?"

"Not yet, Daddy. We wanted to talk with you and Mother first," Wendy answered quickly. "And we still need to talk with his family."

"What do you think they will say?" her father asked directly of Peter.

"I don't know," Peter admitted, trying hard to meet the man's gaze. "I haven't seen them in over two years. But I doubt they would object."

Then followed a period of questions about his family. He tried, without going into much detail, to briefly explain the estrangement that existed between him and his adopted parents. At last they seemed satisfied. Again there was a long silence as hopes, dreams, and expectations raced around the room.

"Well, mother," Wendy's father spoke at last, turning to the woman who sat quietly beside him on the couch. "What do you think?"

"Is there any way we can get you to change your mind?" she asked them. "Maybe give it some more time and finish school first?"

"No, Mother," Wendy answered without hesitation.

"Well, there's our answer," she conceded, looking at her husband. "It really doesn't look like we have much to say about it. They have made up their minds." Turning back to Peter and Wendy, she smiled warmly. "I think we should give them our blessing and welcome Peter into the family!"

"So be it," her husband agreed.

A cheer went up from the sisters, who had watched patiently and silently. The room then erupted into excited chatter as plans for the wedding got under way.

Wendy's father made it clear it should be soon. He saw no reason for a couple to wait very long after making a commitment to each other. Waiting only increased the chance of the relationship getting out of hand before its time. Better to get on with it.

The date was set for December 19, less than twelve weeks away, and only a week after the fall semester of school would be completed and the last game of the season played. But already Peter was impatient. He could not wait until at long last he would have someone who really and for all time would belong to him.

Sixteen

Those hectic months between October and December were some of the happiest and most fulfilling days of Peter's adult life. It was a time filled with challenge and expectancy. For the first time in his life, every part of him was being directed toward some positive and constructive goal. He was beginning to sense that not only could there be a goal in life, but that living itself has its rewards. Not all of life was imbued with pain and suffering. It felt strange to be working *toward* something rather than running away from everything.

Although they were demanding and time consuming, he loved his college classes. Through their challenge to his intellect he began to perceive a world of possibilities far beyond, but no less real than his own. Exposure to new ideas deepened his resolve to know and understand more. He intended to graduate with a degree.

Then there was his work with the kids. His heart was being challenged to expand beyond its own need to include the needs of others, to care as much about the lives of the kids as about his own.

Most frightening of all was the challenge to his spiritual self, the real person dwelling tentatively somewhere within the shell of physical appearances. This was the greatest challenge of all, in that it tested his belief in the fundamental goodness of all God's creation—himself, his belief in the ideal of genuine love, and his willingness to risk his humanness in a union with another person. Did he still have the capacity to trust another person with his life? Dare he care? Even more important, would it be possible to alter the legacy of his childhood so his distorted self-image could include the personal sense of adequacy necessary to maintain such a relationship? And then there was God. Could God truly be trusted to know what He was doing with Peter's life? To trust another to pilot your ship, particularly in a storm, took a faith Peter was not sure he had.

These and a thousand similar thoughts flooded his every waking moment during those months. Despite his uncertainties, he vowed to begin each day as he closed out the last—filled with hope and gratitude that he was blessed with yet one more day!

The week following the announcement of their engagement, two significant events occurred in Peter's life. The Avenue Panthers football team played its first game, and Wendy was taken to meet Peter's adopted parents.

Unsure why, Peter was possessed by a nagging urge to share the news of his engagement with his parents. Although he could not know it, let alone admit it at the time, that urge was rooted in the still-present infantile need to win their acceptance and approval. At some level of consciousness, he believed if they could see what a quality person Wendy was, that she could love him enough to marry him, then maybe they would see he was not as bad as they had thought, and just maybe—maybe they could love him too.

Wendy was with him in his apartment as he dialed the familiar number. The phone rang several times before he heard his mother's cheerful voice.

"Hello?"

Again, after years of no contact, her voice sent waves of powerful emotions pulsating through him. His mouth felt so dry he was not sure he could speak.

"Mom? This is Peter," he said at last, uncertain of her reaction. Wendy was watching him closely.

There was a long silence at the other end. Peter could almost see her face and the displeasure that must surely be registered there. He began regretting that he had called.

"Well, hello, son!" she said at last. Her voice was warm and inviting. "It has been a long time. Where have you been keeping yourself?"

"I'm in school now, Mom, and working," he answered, hoping this would please her.

"Well, that's fine, son! I'm proud of you."

She was proud of him?! How long had it been since he had heard those words from anybody, let alone his mother? Suddenly the yearning for her approval deepened into an obsession.

"Mom, there's something I need to talk over with you and Dad. Is there any chance I can come over in the next day or two?" he asked.

"Well sure, son. Any time." Her voice was still bright and cheerful, but now there was a hint of caution in it. "What's the matter, you need some money?"

"No, Mom, I don't need money. It's something else. And it's really important."

"Well, if it's that important, why don't you come on over now? Dad and I aren't doing anything special at the moment." Peter hesitated and looked quickly at Wendy. She was watching him.

"Can we go right now?" he silently mouthed the words. She nodded.

"That would be great, Mom!"

"Are you in trouble with the law, Peter?" she asked warily. "If you are, there isn't much we can do to help you, you know. It's like we've always told you. You're responsible for your own actions. You make your own bed and you have to lie in it!"

Peter felt sick. Memories of other lectures given in the middle of the night during beatings flooded back into his consciousness. Suddenly he had to get away from that voice.

"No, Mom. It's nothing like that. I'll see you in a little while."

Peter used the time in the shower to regain his composure. The nausea had vanished and the knot in his stomach had relaxed a little. Again and again he reminded himself that they could no longer hurt him. He was now as big, if not bigger, than they.

By the time he stepped out of the shower Peter had pumped himself into an attitude of near-defiance. He reveled in the fantasy of a physical confrontation between

173

him and his parents, when he would once-and-for-all show them they could no longer do to him what they had done when he was a child. He was as tough, as strong, and as mean as they!

"They had better not mess with me!" he blurted as they got into the car. Wendy was strangely silent as they made the short drive. Peter hardly noticed. He was preoccupied with preparing himself for the meeting.

Parking in the driveway behind his father's company car, Peter hurriedly lit a cigarette. The house looked about the same. The trim had been painted another color, and the trees and shrubs were larger than he remembered. Taking a deep breath, he fought to hold the feeling of bravado that had carried him to this point.

They got out of the car and walked toward the stone steps leading up to the front porch. The last time he had used those steps was the night his father had thrown him bodily down them with the command never to return. Peter became aware of a dull ache at the base of his skull.

He pulled Wendy close beside him as they stood poised to ring the doorbell and flashed her a reassuring smile he hoped appeared more confident than he felt. The door opened before the chimes had finished their melodic announcement.

For the first time in more than two years, Peter stood face to face with his adopted mother. She was wearing a brightly flowered kimono that made her smile appear that much brighter. For a split second he saw the curiosity in her bright blue eyes as she looked squarely at him. But just as suddenly it was gone and her eyes were dancing their welcome from him to Wendy and back again. Peter felt his self-assurance melt away in the warmth of her presence. How many times had he searched those same eyes for some sign of love, or caring, or understanding, or at the very least, mercy?

"Hello, stranger!" she said. "It's about time you came home to visit your old mom and dad!"

Peter felt as limp as an old, wet rag. This was too good to be true! It was more than he had hoped for, and yet all that he had hoped for. She actually seemed pleased to see him.

"Hello, Mom," he said awkwardly. Suddenly remembering Wendy, he lost no time introducing her. "Mom, this is Wendy."

"Hello, Wendy!" she greeted her just as warmly. "You all come on in."

They were escorted into the house, past the living room, past the stairs leading downstairs to the den and upstairs to the bedrooms, and straight into the kitchen. Peter's father was sitting at the table with a cup of coffee in front of him.

"Hello, Dad," Peter greeted his father. He kept his distance, but extended his hand. Looking closely, he found the finely chiseled features of his father as immutable as he remembered them. As always, it was impossible to guess what he was thinking.

After everyone was seated and given something to drink, Peter's parents began asking him about his schoolwork and his job. Cautiously at first, for fear of saying or doing something that would break the spell, but then more enthusiastically as he saw they were genuinely interested, Peter told them of his classes and how much he was enjoying them. He took long minutes to describe the kids at the school and his hopes for them through the athletic program. Wendy sat patiently through the reunion.

After a while the conversation stalled. It was then his father asked the question.

"So, what is it you wanted to talk to us about?"

Although the question was innocent enough, Peter immediately recognized the undertone of threat. It was a hidden message that warned Peter not to expect a positive response to whatever it was he had to say. The signal was clear: Do not put them on the spot!

Clearing his throat, Peter looked at Wendy for reassurance and then back at his parents. Frantically he sought the words he needed. Then suddenly, out of nowhere, as though it were not even his own voice, he heard himself speaking.

"Can Wendy and I get married?"

Peter was mortified. Overcome with his own humiliation, he could not look them in the eye. Why did he have to say it that way? It sounded like a child asking permission to go out and play, or for a cookie, or a hug. It reminded him of the time he had lived under their absolute control and dared not be assertive for fear of their retaliatory anger and violence. The nausea returned as he felt again that all-encompassing fear. What had happened to him? He had come not to ask if he could get married, but to tell them that he was!

They picked up on it immediately.

"Why are you bothering to ask us?" The smile was now gone from his mother's lips. "Aren't you man enough to make your own decisions?"

The question cut through him like a knife. Something stirred deep inside, and as it swelled, Peter found himself staring directly into the eyes staring at him.

"As a matter of fact, I am!" His voice was low and his mouth barely moved.

"So why ask us if you can get married if you are such a big man?" his father repeated the question.

"Out of courtesy and respect for you as my parents," Peter answered just as quickly. His eyes met and held those of his father.

"Hah! Since when did you have any respect for us?" his mother burst out. "And courtesy? That's a laugh. Who are you trying to fool?" She paused for a moment to look hard at Peter. "Still playing con games, aren't you, little man?"

It was all Peter could do to keep from bursting into tears. His intentions were once again being totally misunderstood. Desperately, he had hoped it would be different this time! That they would listen without criticizing or humiliating. That they would understand, give their support and acceptance, and be proud of him. But it was just like all the other times. Nothing had changed. Nothing at all.

"No, I'm not playing games," he somehow managed to say. "Wendy and I are getting married whether you give your permission or not. But we had hoped you would give us your blessing." There! He had said it the right way! That is what he had meant to say from the beginning.

"Well, why didn't you say that in the first place?" his mother retorted.

"All we really wanted was your approval," softly, Wendy spoke for the first time.

For a moment Peter's parents looked at Wendy. Then Peter noticed the hardness of their faces begin to soften until at last his mother's smile returned. But the swelling inside him was still there. More than anger, it was now a burning, consuming rage.

"Well, you kids are old enough to know what you want," his mother spoke unemotionally. To Wendy, she continued, "Frankly, though, I don't think Peter is mature enough to be getting married. But that is your problem now. I tried for seven years to help him grow up, and look at him. Obviously, I failed. But maybe you are a better woman than me. Maybe you can make him grow up!" There was a hint of disgust in her eyes as her gaze returned to Peter.

That did it! The swelling was now out of control. Bursting with rage, Peter placed his hands on the table and slowly pushed his way to his feet.

"I don't have to sit here and listen to your b--- s---!" he grated through clenched teeth. Smiling coldly at his mother with his lips curled back, he leaned forward and spoke directly to her. "And just for the record, I grew up more in my first week on the street than I ever did in this house! At least out there I didn't have to worry about getting the h--- beat out of me every time I turned around!"

Defiantly Peter looked from his mother to his father. He could see the reaction forming in the man's set jaw and clenched fists.

"What's the matter, Dad? You don't like to hear the truth? Or maybe you want to hit me again like you used to. Is that it?" Part of him wanted his dad to hit him. This time, he would hit back!

"Come on, Peter!" Wendy was pulling on his arm. "We better go now."

His parents made no move to stop them or show them to the door. They sat strangely silent and unmoving.

"If it's all right, I'll call you in a few days to discuss the wedding plans," Wendy called out as they neared the front door. There was no answer.

Wendy tried to calm him down as they drove away. He was far more upset than she.

"You have not seen each other for a couple of years, Peter. You can't expect everything to change overnight. It takes time," she tried to explain. "They don't even know you, now that you're an adult. Give them a chance. They are just going to have to realize you are not a child anymore."

Fortunately, Peter did not have much time to think about it at that moment. The Panthers' first game was the next day. He had to begin thinking about the team and how they were going to win.

Only occasionally during that evening and while working in the classroom the following morning did Peter remember their visit with his parents. When he did, he felt an overwhelming sadness at the way they had treated him and an equal sense of amazement at the way he had reacted.

Right after lunch Peter gathered the members of the football team in the empty room off the cafeteria. He was pleased that most of the players had passed the eligibility check that morning—all but two.

It was hard to tell those two they would have to watch the game from the sidelines, but in order for the program to succeed, it had to be done. He shared their disappointment and promised to try to help them get their grades up so they could play in the next game.

The school they were playing was located across town in a middle-class neighborhood. It was a large school with an enrollment of over a thousand. Peter watched from the window as busload after busload of kids and teachers were deposited in the parking lot and made their way to the field.

Then came the visiting team. They had twice as many players, and the size of several of the boys left a sinking feeling in the pit of Peter's stomach. They looked awesome! Dressed in bright red uniforms with white numbers and their names on the back, they looked to Peter like a swarm of big red ants spilling across the playing field.

His own team did not have game uniforms. They would have to play in practice pants and jerseys. Peter knew the contrast between the two teams would be incredibly embarrassing. It was then he vowed that his boys were going to have bright new uniforms. Somehow. But he would think about that after the game. Right now he had his hands full.

All the students and faculty were dismissed to attend the game. They seemed small in number compared to the horde of cheering visitors on the other side of the field.

After final words of instruction, Peter led his team through the double line of cheerleaders, with Tami as their captain, waiting for them. Once on the field he had them jog all around the sideline, passing directly in front of the opposing team.

"I want them to get a good look at the faces of the team that is going to whip them!" he had told the boys. Peter was proud as they jogged, one by one, past the catcalls of the visitors without even once breaking stride or being lured into a confrontation. Just a few weeks ago, there surely would have been a free-for-all.

"They may be prettier than we are," he told the boys as his team huddled around him, "but we're tougher, and a better football team! You don't win ball games with pretty clothes."

The visiting team kicked off to the Panthers. Taking the ball on their own seventeen-yard line, the Panthers marched the full length of the field to score in eight plays! The home crowd went wild.

Peter could not believe the ease with which his team had

scored. It was 6-0 after the Panthers failed on their extra-point try.

The rest of the game was a stalemate. The Panther defense, with sensational plays, again and again thwarted the visitors' attempts to score. Timid, self-conscious Ronnie, who would not look anyone in the eye, came alive and played like a cornered bobcat. He recorded eight quarterback sacks and twice as many assists.

But the Panthers could not score again either. With less than a minute left in the game, Peter was drenched with sweat. He had tried everything he could think of to set up another score. But nothing worked. It had turned into an incredible defensive struggle. By then he attributed their opening drive score more to luck than to skill.

It was fourth down, with only a minute left in the game. Peter had three options. They could run the ball, probably pick up the necessary yardage for a first down, and let the clock run out. He ruled this out because the other team had time-outs left and had all but stopped their running game. They could kick the ball on fourth down. But this was what the other team was expecting, and it also set up the possibility of a long runback. Peter chose the third option. The Panthers would try to catch the visitors off guard with a fourth-down pass.

The cheerleaders for both teams had kept the crowd whipped into a frenzy all afternoon, and Danny, the quarterback, could barely hear Peter's instructions as he outlined the play. Paul was to go straight down the right sideline, and Danny was to take the ball from the center, roll to his right, and throw the pass as far as he could. Paul would run under it for the catch.

The visitors seemed confused because the Panthers were not kicking on fourth down, and Danny hurried the count before they had a chance to adjust their defense. Peter could hear one of the visiting coaches screaming from across the field.

Then in slow motion, the play unfolded before Peter's

eyes. Every muscle in his body was tense. He held his breath, his eyes riveted on every detail.

Danny took the snap from the center as the two lines of players crashed into each other. Paul took off like a bolt of lightning. Danny rolled to the right behind his backfield, which formed a wall ahead of him. Then, with his eyes glued on Paul, Danny pulled his arm back and threw the ball. It seemed to hang in the air for an eternity before a pair of hands closed around it.

The triumphant yell that started in Peter's throat died a split second later when he realized the hands that had grabbed the ball were white. Paul's were black. A streaking defender had intercepted the pass and was now racing down the unprotected sideline toward the Panther goal line. It had happened so fast his own players did not have time to react. The visitors scored the tying touchdown with only seconds left on the clock.

Stunned, the home crowd was silent. The visitors lined up on the Panther two-yard line for the extra-point try. If they made it, they would win. The most Peter could hope for now was to block that extra point and settle for a tie.

He called a red-dog defense, which put all eleven players on the line of scrimmage. They had to stop the visitors!

The opposing quarterback took the snap, twisted around, and handed the ball to an end racing to the right. The Panther defense read the play well and moved laterally along the line of scrimmage, setting up an impenetrable wall between the ball carrier and the goal line.

Again Peter was about to cheer, feeling sure his defense would tackle the ball carrier short of the goal line. But just as the boy was about to reach the line of Panther defenders, he suddenly stopped dead in his tracks and threw the ball back across the field.

There, with not a Panther defender within ten yards, stood the visiting quarterback in the end zone. He caught the ball and the game was over. The final score was 7-6. The Avenue Panthers had lost.

Seventeen

Throughout the weekend Peter could think of nothing but the loss of the Panther game. It was a personal defeat more bitter than any he had yet experienced. He had failed. Not only had he let the school down, but he also had betrayed the team. The boys trusted him to know what he was doing, to coach them and call the plays, in the belief that he could show them how to become winners. What a joke! How could a loser possibly show anyone how to be a winner?

He spent the weekend deeply depressed. Over and over, he replayed the final minute of the game in his mind's eye. If only he had not called the pass play! How he wished he could take back that moment. The boys and the cheerleaders had done their part. They had been fantastic! *He* was the one who could not measure up when it really counted! Peter was sure the student population hated him now. His incompetence must be the talk of the neighborhood!

Fully convinced everyone at the school now knew just how inadequate he really was and would no longer want him around the kids, Peter made his way slowly to the school on Monday morning, prepared to submit his resignation.

Mrs. Parks did not smile as he entered the principal's office. With eyes that hid what he knew she must be thinking, she said, "Dr. Campbell wants to see you in the teacher's lounge. Now!"

His feet feeling as though they were encased in solid lead, Peter left the office without a word and made his way painfully to the teacher's lounge. Fighting guilt and shame, he paused at the door to take a deep breath before facing Dr. Campbell. He knew he deserved whatever the principal said or did.

Unable to avoid the inevitable, he opened the door and stepped tentatively inside. He was shocked to see the room filled with people. Every teacher in the school was there, along with the parents of several football players. Even some of the parents had come to see him fired!

An overwhelming urge to run and hide took hold of him. But just as he was about to turn toward the door, he was stopped dead in his tracks. Softly at first, then louder and with more vigor, the people were clapping as though applauding someone special. And beginning to rise to their feet.

Peter was astonished and confused. What is going on here? he wondered as he fought to understand.

After a moment the applause faded. Peter searched the sea of smiling faces for some explanation. At last Dr. Campbell took shape out of the crowd.

"You left so quickly after the game Friday that none of us had a chance to thank you."

"To thank me?" Peter's voice squeaked in disbelief.

"That was one of the most fantastic games I have ever seen!" exclaimed one of the male teachers. "I wish we had it on videotape."

"But . . . but . . . but we lost!" Peter whispered.

"Don't you have any idea what really happened last Friday, Peter?" Dr. Campbell asked quickly. "Sure! It would have been nice to have the final score in our favor. But the final score was not nearly as important as what happened on the field and in the stands. Don't you see?" He continued when Peter still did not seem to understand. "For the first time since I have been here, black kids, white kids, and Spanish-American kids were all playing *together* rather than fighting. Everywhere I looked last Friday—on the field, at the cheerleaders, in the stands, everywhere—I saw black, white, and brown faces all mixed together. For the first time ever, we were united for a common purpose. That is a major achievement in this community!"

Peter was stunned. Nothing like this had ever happened to him before. It was beyond his wildest dreams. It was hard for him to believe he could actually lose the game and still everybody would be proud of him.

Peter did not know it then, but his willingness to return to the school that day was a significant step forward. Although he had felt certain the principal would dismiss him, his commitment to the kids and his work there was strong enough to give him the courage to show up, though every sense screamed for him to flee, to admit defeat, to abort the effort.

But he was not fired. Instead, he had won the applause and respect of the school and community. Moreover, that game was the only one the Avenue Panthers would lose during the entire two years Peter worked at the school! After two seasons, the Panthers' football team boasted a record of twenty-three wins and only one loss. It was an incredible achievement for a group of undisciplined, racially tense and volatile young people. They became winners, confident and self-assured, proud to belong to something greater than themselves, but something that could not have been without them. It was theirs and they were it!

The winning ways of the kids at Avenue School did not end with the games. Students bored with school and frustrated with its many demands for performance took a new interest in their studies; they passed exams, did their reading and homework. They knew that failing a grade check would mean sitting out a game. And that was a price too high to pay! With the help of a couple of other faculty members, Peter was able to bring specialists from the community into the school to teach the kids such things as basic hygiene, etiquette, and manners. The girls were given an opportunity to learn about dress and makeup, and the modeling-school instructor also discussed dating and sex. Peter made sure Tami attended this program.

So it was that Peter was feeling good about his work and achievements as December 1970 reached its midpoint. The football team had closed out its first season with only one loss, and he had passed all his final exams, which was no small accomplishment. He had successfully completed his first semester of college and had twelve semester hours toward an Associate of Arts degree. It felt like money in the bank.

Then came that special day. December 19. A Saturday. The day dawned bright and clear, one of the finest Mother Nature had to offer. Driving along Telegraph Road on his way to the church later in the afternoon, Peter could see the ocean spread endlessly along the shore in a rough, twisting line. The water was shimmering in the sunlight. Seeing it lying there had a calming effect, as it always did, upon his eager but anxious emotions.

There were only a couple of cars in the parking lot when Peter arrived at the church. He was an hour early. On purpose. He wanted some time alone, to think, before the service began.

Several women working in the dimly lit church did not notice him as he slipped into the last pew. One woman was at the altar, arranging and rearranging, to suit her precise taste, the huge bouquets of white carnations at each end of the altar and on the floor on each side. Beside the altar flowers were ornate candelabra, each holding eight candles. The eucharistic vessels sat in the center, directly under the large wooden cross suspended from the pointed roof.

Two other women were slowly making their way down the aisle, attaching seven-foot candles to the sides of each pew. To these were fastened large white satin bows, in striking contrast to the deep burgundy carpet.

After a while, Peter's eyes were drawn to the cross above the altar. How many times during the past few years had he sat in this very same pew and looked at that cross? It had to be hundreds. But he never seemed to tire of it. There was something mysterious and profoundly mystical about the cross. How could the very object of one man's torture and death be a symbol of hope for millions of others? And why was it that in less than an hour he and Wendy would stand in its shadow to be married, while a whole body of people gathered around it to watch?

Peter toyed with these thoughts as the passing time swept him ever closer to the appointed hour. He knew Wendy was already there, buried somewhere in the massive structure, shut off from unnecessary eyes and ears as she made her final preparations. He had not seen her since noon the preceding day when her mother had chased him out of the house with the command not to see Wendy again until the wedding.

For a long time Peter let his thoughts dwell luxuriously upon Wendy. He had never met a nicer, more thoughtful person in all his life. She would do anything to help another. She was so good, and attractive, and intelligent. She would never do the things he had done in his life. And she loved him? How could someone so perfect love someone so . . . suspect? Peter's awe and respect were so great, the thought of her as his wife seemed strange, even bizarre. There was no doubt in his mind that he was getting the better deal! A deep humility filled him. He wished he had more to offer her, although he was not sure what that might be. It just seemed she was not getting much in the deal—just him.

Groups of people beginning to enter the church recalled Peter from his thoughts. It was time to get ready. He felt relaxed as he stood up from the pew to go to the dressing room.

It was not until he heard the music that he began to tense and get nervous. By the time he and his best man, a fellow student from school, had taken up their positions just inside the sacristy door, Peter could hardly stand still. The more his friend tried to calm him, the more anxious he became. What am I doing here? a voice deep inside his brain screamed. Are you crazy? Get out while you still can!

The wedding march began! It was too late to run now. He had to go through with it! This was their cue to enter the church and take their positions at the bottom of the steps leading into the chancel.

"Are you ready?" he croaked through parched lips to the equally nervous man behind him.

"If you are!" came the answer.

"Got the ring?" Peter asked for the hundredth time.

"Right here!" his best man assured him.

"My tie straight?" Peter asked as he turned to face the man.

"Quit stalling and get out there!" the man exclaimed under his breath as he reached around Peter and opened the door. Peter was met by a sea of faces that all seemed to blend together into one blur of hair and skin. They were looking at him! Peter felt sure he was going to faint. But somehow, with a strength not his own, he made it to his position.

Father Paul was already there, standing pontifically at the top of the steps with the closed prayer book in the crook of his arm. He was wearing a white alb, cinctured snugly with rope at the waist, an ornately knitted white stole, and a large silver cross. He smiled as Peter approached. Peter tried to return the smile but could manage only a grimace he was sure the priest would think concealed a groan.

But Father Paul did not seem to notice. Instead he looked away from Peter and nodded his head slightly toward the rear of the church. Peter followed his gaze, then turned with the rest of the congregation now standing to watch the entrance of the bride.

What Peter saw left him stunned. The most beautiful woman he had ever seen was walking down the aisle toward him on the arm of some man he assumed was her father. He could not take his eyes off her long enough to find out for sure. Suddenly all the worry, doubt, and tension flowed from his mind and body, leaving his legs feeling like Jello. How could anyone not love someone so beautiful?

At last the march ended and she was with him at the foot of the steps. But the man still stood between them. They faced the priest together, and the service began.

"Dearly beloved, we are gathered together here in the sight of God . . . to join together this man and this woman . . . " Father Paul began in his most commanding voice.

Peter's mind wandered to the vision of loveliness beside him. He was tempted to reach across her father and take her hand to make sure she was real, to confirm to his doubting senses that this was really happening and not just a dream.

"Who gives this woman . . . " continued Father Paul, cutting into Peter's thoughts.

"Her mother and I do," barked the familiar voice between them.

As her father stepped back to join the family in the first pew, Father Paul took Wendy's right hand and placed it in Peter's. Now it was just the two of them before the priest. He led them, accompanied by the maid of honor and best man, to the altar rail, where vows and rings were exchanged. Then followed their private Communion, just the two of them kneeling before the priest. Most of it was lost on Peter. His mind was filled with the woman kneeling beside him.

At last the priest bid the pair stand up. He wrapped his stole around their clasped hands and held them firmly as he looked past them at the congregation.

"And now, by the power invested in me by Almighty God and this state, I now pronounce you man and wife!"

Hardly had the words left his throat when the cheer rose out of the congregation. So loud was it that Peter hardly heard the priest tell him he could now kiss the bride.

The kiss was short-lived, though, because he and Wendy were swamped by a mob of kids pouring out of the pews. Peter's shock at this unexpected display of exuberance faded quickly, replaced with pure delight, when he discovered who the kids were. The entire Panther football team and cheering squad had come to the wedding! There was no one in all the world he would rather have had there than those kids—except for his two brothers.

Excited and chattering, the youngsters escorted the two down the aisle and out of the church to the parish hall where the reception was to be held. Once inside, it did not take them long to find the cake and other goodies. Dressed in their very best—for most, tennis shoes, blue jeans, and sport shirt—the kids looked great. Peter was so proud of them!

But that was not the only surprise. His adopted mother and father were there! He had never been sure they would come and had prepared himelf for disappointment. But he was even more excited by who they had brought with them!

Straggling behind with sheepish self-conscious grins, in their Marine Corps dress blues, including white gloves, came his two brothers! Although he had invited them, Peter had been convinced they would not be able to get leave. But here they were! Both of them. Peter was ecstatic.

Peter and Wendy stayed at the reception for an hour, visiting with the people who had come to offer their best wishes. When it was time to leave, Peter felt a momentary pang as he once again said good-bye to his brothers. He had no idea when he might see them again. With the constant need for more men in Vietnam, that might be never.

Hugging them both, he finally dragged himself away and took Wendy's waiting hand. Together they made a wild dash to the car through a shower of rice. Peter helped Wendy into the front seat, and as he moved around the car to the driver's side, he could not help noticing the golden sunset spread in dazzling panorama along the horizon. For a moment he was sure it was there just for him. He paused long enough to appreciate its majestic beauty and thank God for it, for Wendy, and for making him the happiest man on the face of earth.

BREAKING
THE
CYCLE

Eighteen

Wendy and I moved into a small apartment on the beach, with the ocean only a few hundred feet outside our front door. It was a perfect place to begin our life together. Much of our free time was spent walking hand in hand in the sun, sand, and surf, talking and enjoying belonging to each other. We went to sleep to the sound of the crashing surf, constantly reminding us that nothing had changed with the coming of darkness. I liked that! Even more, I needed it.

After the expected ups and downs of adjusting to the intimacy and expectations of living with another person, we settled into a routine. To make ends meet, Wendy worked in a dress shop and I continued my work at the school, while we both kept up our classes at the college. Although infrequently, we also attended Father Paul's church on Sunday mornings. Father Paul became a very special friend to us, and later a key factor in some major life decisions I had to make.

Given the awesome task of finishing school and establishing careers, we decided to wait a couple of years before having children. That would also give us a chance to enjoy each other before assuming responsibility for another human life. Although we openly acknowledged our desire to have children eventually, the thought of becoming a father terrified me. The only thing I knew about being a father was how to use fear, force, and intimidation to control any innocent little lives given into my care. Discipline and

193

control were one and the same, as far as I knew. It would be several years before I learned just how dangerous and painful it is to confuse the two.

What if I could not be a good father? What if my children did not like me or grew up to hate me? Or what if I did to them what my adopted father had done to me? These and similar thoughts filled me with nausea and fear. I was grateful we could agree to wait. Besides, I already had kids—the kids at the school. I really did not know how much they had come to mean to me until the night of the banquet.

After completing our first season with a record of eleven wins and one loss, and with half the cheerleaders and team members graduating to their next level of education, I did not know what to expect of the squads we would assemble for the 1971 season. But if the 1970 team was outstanding, the team the following year was nothing less than awesome! Six of the teams they faced that year could not score a single point. Those that did score were able to amass a combined total of only 56 points, while the Panther offense rolled up close to 350, on their way to an undefeated season!

Knowing my tenure as coach was over, I wanted to do something really special for these outstanding kids, something that would be a lifetime reminder of their success. I got together with a group of very excited and proud parents, and we decided to hold fund-raisers to provide the boys and girls with an awards banquet. And that we did! We sold candy, washed cars, had paper and bottle drives, and in a very short time had the money we needed.

The banquet was scheduled for a Saturday night. Dr. Campbell had graciously donated the food out of the school's cafeteria budget, and several of the cafeteria staff volunteered their time and energy to prepare and serve it. We were delighted!

Gathering the squad of players and the cheerleaders together for our last meeting several days before the banquet, I told them what we were doing and why. Although none of them had ever attended a banquet, I will never forget the happiness and pride that blazed in those young eyes.

Slowly and carefully, I explained to them what I expected. Although the banquet was being held in their honor, all parents and siblings were invited. One of the kids asked if it was OK to bring just one parent, because that was all he had. Another asked who they should bring if they had no parents at all. This boy was living in a foster home. A third asked if it was OK for them to come even if their parents would not.

"Bring who you have," I encouraged them. "If you do not have anyone who will come, then you come and sit with me at my table."

After resolving other concerns, we moved on. I told them I wanted them to dress in the very best clothes they had. No tennis shoes or blue jeans if they had something nicer. If not, blue jeans and tennis shoes were acceptable. The girls were told to wear dresses, if possible. I also told them I wanted them all to bathe, comb their hair, and be on their very best behavior throughout the evening.

I arrived early to begin setting up for the banquet and was barely finished when people began to arrive. I watched with unimaginable pride as the kids came in one by one. All the girls had their hair neatly done and wore dresses. Some of the boys actually wore suits; others, slacks and sport shirts. All wore brightly scrubbed and smiling faces. There was not a pair of blue jeans or tennis shoes to be seen anywhere in the room! I learned later that several of the parents had used much-needed money to buy their children slacks and shoes from local thrift shops.

They were undoubtedly the best-looking group of young people I had ever seen! Even Dr. Campbell and the teachers who came were amazed that these were the same children who filled the seats in their classrooms every day. I think the kids earned a new measure of respect for themselves and for one another. Perhaps more important, the teachers began to see in those kids new possibilities beyond their usual expectations.

After dinner, I did the hardest and most pleasurable thing in my adult life. I got up on stage in front of a cafeteria full of people looking at me! Only my love for the kids and a courage not my own gave me the strength to do that.

Starting with the girls, each cheerleader was introduced by name and invited to come up on stage. Once there, I summarized her performance for the year, just as I did for each of the boys. As I talked about each child, a photographer would snap our picture as we stood with our arms around each other. Then I would hand the child his or her trophy. Each girl also was awarded a necklace with a megaphone, and each of the boys was given a game jersey with his name and "1971 Champions" emblazoned across the front and back. All of them stayed on stage until the last person had received the awards.

Throughout their lives, these kids might never have another opportunity to go up on a stage in front of their parents, friends, and an entire room full of people, even their teachers, to be praised for their achievements and receive an award, amidst applause intended just for them. I wanted it to last as long as possible. I wanted each of them to remember it! No matter where they might end up in life, I wanted them to remember a time when they were really something special and knew it.

Just as I was about to ask for a final round of applause for the boys and girls standing proudly on the stage, Dr. Campbell stepped forward, accompanied by a woman I did not at first recognize. Together, they came up the steps. The woman was carrying a trophy. As they walked into the light, I suddenly recognized her. It was Tami's mother!

Coming with Dr. Campbell to the microphone, she looked first at the audience and then back at me.

"On behalf of the parents, the teachers, the community, and all the children, we want you to have this as our way of saying thank you for all you have done for our kids!" She handed me the trophy and stood on tiptoe to kiss me lightly on the cheek.

I wish I could share with you the feeling I had at that moment. All my life I had been told I was such a worthless human being that I really had no right even to be alive. And now this woman was standing in front of a room full of people and thanking me? She even kissed me! Me, of all people. For what? Caring? I was so filled with joy and confusion, at first I did not even notice the thunderous applause as everyone in the room rose.

I was so overcome by emotion I could not even go to the microphone and thank them. It was all I could do to keep from breaking into tears. Instead, I dropped to one knee and called all the kids around me so all in the room could have one last look at the 1971 Champions, the greatest group of young people to ever come out of that school.

I do not know where any of those kids are today. They are young adults now. Maybe with families of their own. But I hope they remember that night as I do. What started as an attempt to give them a moment in their lives they would never forget turned out to be one of the most memorable moments of *my* life. I shall never forget that moment, or them.

I left the school at the end of that academic year, in June 1972, the same month I graduated from junior college with an Associate of Arts degree. At the encouragement of several professors and Wendy, I had applied for admission into one of the smaller state colleges and miraculously had been accepted.

An opportunity to earn a Bachelor's Degree was more than I had ever dreamed possible. Again, I was both excited and ridden with fear that I might fail. But despite my fears, I knew I had to try.

At that time a dream began to form in my mind. I decided to take courses that would qualify me to become a teacher. Then I would teach my way through law school, hoping I could help pass laws to protect other children from the horrible abuse I had experienced. I was naive enough to think that child abuse was a legal problem—a problem that could be stopped by the courts and prevented by passing laws. But that was my plan. I declared an English major, and a teaching and psychology minor.

The next two years were very difficult. I was able to find a job in a fast-food restaurant. The four-to-midnight shift was the only one available, but that was just as well. It kept my mornings free for classes.

Working and going to school full time is a heavy load. Most days, I would be gone from home from eight in the morning until midnight. I had very little free time. When I was home I was either very tired, asleep, or trying to study or write one of the endless papers required by my classes. Sadly, there was little time to be a husband and companion for Wendy. As days grew into weeks and weeks into months, I began to sense an estrangement between us. Although it concerned me, I was too preoccupied to think much about it. Instead, we had a baby.

Our daughter, Deanna, was born early on the morning of April 22, 1973—Easter morning, to be exact. I practically fainted when the nurse finally came to the waiting room, where Wendy's family and I had paced away the hours, to tell us it was a girl. The joy, happiness, relief, and fear were almost more than I could bear. She was the most beautiful baby in the whole world! It took only a moment to fall head over heels in love with her.

Later that night I went home and wrote my new daughter a letter. I do not remember now all I said in the letter. But I do remember telling her I would always love her and would never leave her and that no matter what she might do or become as she grew, she would always be my princess, and I would never stop loving her. Completing the letter, I signed and dated it, sealed it, and put it away for safekeeping. I still have that unopened letter, now twelve years old. It is my intention to give it to her on her eighteenth birthday.

Two weeks after Deanna's arrival, I was fired from my job. A new, single, and very ambitious manager had taken over the business. It was his stated goal to be the youngest district manager in the company. In an attempt to impress the existing district manager by cutting payroll costs, a fellow employee and I were released. From his perspective, I was the logical one to go. Having been there more than a year and a half, I had long since become the assistant manager, drawing the highest hourly wage of any employee—a smashing three dollars an hour!

A strange thing happened after he told me I was being released. I invited him to dinner that night! Then an even stranger thing happened: He accepted! The true irony of that situation did not strike me until much later. What drove me to open my home and share a meal with the very man who, not hours before, had deprived me and my family of the means for providing tomorrow's meal? It was incredible! But strangely, to this day I do not regret having done it.

A few weeks later I was able to get a job making collections for a finance company. It was terrible work, but it paid our way through my last semester of college.

In June 1974, I graduated with a Bachelor's Degree in English. Still unsure of myself and not willing to take the risk of being rejected by a law school, I went to work for a company that specialized in estate and financial planning. I had to pass exams for a securities license, as well as for licenses to sell insurance and annuities. Although I enjoyed the estate-planning portion of the work, I hated the selling. Something kept telling me I could be doing something more important with my life than worrying about other people's money!

At about that time, Father Paul shook my world to its very roots.

"Have you ever thought about the priesthood as a vocation?" he asked.

"The priesthood?" I responded in shocked disbelief. Surely he must be joking! Me a priest? The thought was beyond comprehension. Besides, who would want an ex-biker as their minister? The thought was ludicrous.

"Yes," he continued, "the priesthood. I think you would make an exceptional priest. Particularly with your life experience. Of course, it would mean going to seminary."

I dismissed the thought on the spot and went on about my business. But it kept nagging at me, like a voice out of nowhere—calling me, calling me. It would come at times when I least expected it, at times when I needed to be concentrating on what I was doing. It became such a tremendous nuisance that at last I could ignore it no longer. I went to see Father Paul.

Over the next several weeks he and I met irregularly. I asked him about seminary, what it was like, did he think I could pass the courses, what they would expect of me. Eventually I got around to the things that were really bothering me—my troubled history and my present unworthiness.

I will never forget what he did then. It changed my entire outlook on the church and my place in it. Father Paul handed me a Bible, and during the next hour, I read about one major biblical character after another—in particular, Abraham, Saul, and David. As he talked about each one in turn, I came to realize, as was his intent, that these were not mystical, superhuman beings. These were real men, with real problems, who made real mistakes and had real weaknesses. Each of them did some very bad things. And yet each had a very special place among God's chosen people. Through this demythologizing of Scripture, I came to appreciate and relate to those men in a new and personal way. Not as examples of what I was not and should be, but rather as real people with strengths and weaknesses, just like me.

"Peter," Father Paul said, "if there is a place in God's kingdom for men such as these, then there is a place in God's kingdom for you!"

For days I pondered these words. Not only did they bring me a comforting sense of acceptance, but with that acceptance came an equally profound, though unspoken, challenge. You see, knowing now there was a place for me in that Kingdom compelled me not only to find that place, but to take it! What an incredible and frightening challenge for one who had considered himself a mistake that never should have happened!

The thought haunted me. No matter what I did or where I was, it was there, eating away at the edges of my denial. I became restless and preoccupied, which began to take its toll on my work and everyday life. At a time when all I really wanted was to just be, to just exist in a personal peace, I found no peace.

"How is it you expect to know peace without first knowing purpose?" Father Paul asked me one morning as I tried to explain my trouble. "It is always uncomfortable to stand in the presence of God, knowing that his will and your own are not one and the same. There is no peace except that which comes by uniting the two in a common purpose. God has a wonderful plan for your life, my son. You must seek out that plan and fulfill it!"

The answer came to me in a dream several weeks later. I seemed to be sitting at a table piled with money, in a room full of people waiting their turn to see me. As the people came forward, they handed me money which I placed in one pile. Then from another pile, I gave them more than they had given me. We were all smiling and feeling very pleased with ourselves, while all around us were children, walking, crawling, and lying helplessly on the floor. There were so many that some were being stepped on by the adults waiting in line. Some had cuts and bruises. Others were emaciated and hungry. Some were even bleeding. All were crying, but there was no sound. And all were reaching out with tiny, tentative hands to me and the other adults. But we ignored them, intent on what we were doing. Then I chanced to look at one of them. And what I saw sent me shrieking into the night. It was me! As I looked into my own helpless, desperate eyes, all the fear, pain, and horror of my childhood came rushing back so violently that I vomited.

I could not sleep the rest of that night. I thought and paced and thought and paced until by morning I was an emotional wreck. But there was no doubt left in my mind then. I knew what I had to do.

I waited until eight o'clock and then made my calls. The first was to my employer. Explaining that I was going back to school, I quit my job on the spot. Then I called Father Paul. I knew he would be in his office after conducting morning mass.

"Father Paul," I spoke rapidly into the phone when he answered. "I don't know about becoming a priest, and I don't know what God's will is for my life. But I do know that what I am doing is not it! I want to go to seminary. Will you help me?" There was an urgency in my voice I am sure he did not miss.

"I already have, Peter," he stated matter-of-factly as though he had known all along. "The vestry passed a resolution at our last meeting to sponsor you in seminary."

I was speechless. How had he known? What had prompted him to present me to the vestry for sponsorship even before I had known I wanted to go? This was unreal! Obviously, there was a power greater than my own at work in my life.

In the following weeks I was very busy. First I had to take the Graduate Record Exam required for admission to a graduate school. Then came the psychological exams. Once these were completed and the results in hand, I met with the bishop of the diocese, the commission on ministry, and the diocesan standing committee.

By the end of June, final approval was given. I was going to seminary.

Nineteen

In the spring before we were to leave for seminary, our second child was born. A nine-pound bouncing bundle of boy! Now we had one of each and I was ecstatic. We named him Jonathan for the son of Saul, David's best friend. He was a much-wanted and welcome addition to our family.

Adjusting to a newborn with his endless, necessary demands, while at the same time preparing for our move to another state and the seminary, I became acutely aware of an unresolved and critically important issue. Though my curiosity and desire had increased since the time as a young boy living in foster homes I had vowed to survive until we could be reunited, I had made no real effort to find my older brother and sister or my biological mother and father. Now, I thought, was the time.

With Wendy's support and encouragement, I decided to do just that. At a loss as to where to begin my search, it occurred to me that I remembered the directions to the Jones' farm, which Mrs. Jones had drilled into our heads. I decided to start there. It was a long shot, but I had nothing to lose and everything to gain.

After the long drive across country, it did not take us long to find the farm. The directions I remembered were perfect. A strange feeling came over me as we topped the hill and found the valley before us. For a moment I was again a small boy in the back seat of the sheriff's patrol car, seeing the valley for the first time as the deputy and welfare worker took us to the farm. My curiosity then had been that of a child seeing something new. My curiosity now was of a different sort. I wanted to see where I had been.

Everything looked about the same. The house, barn, smokehouse, chicken house, the corrals, and the wide variety of farm animals.

Although the house was unlocked, there was no one home. I remembered that the Jones never locked their house. For some reason, I never questioned whether they still lived there. Maybe it was the old sewing machine still sitting under the window in the dining room. Or maybe it was the white, badly chipped porcelain mixing bowl I had used to make biscuits. It was sitting on the drainboard beside the sink. Whatever the reason, I was sure I was back.

203

After showing Wendy the bedroom where my brothers and I had shared a bed, I wanted to show her my hiding place under the back porch. But a room had been added to the house. The back porch was gone. I took her to the garden and all over the farm. I even showed her the mulberry tree that had almost claimed my life and the perpetually flowing artesian well where we had drawn up our drinking water.

It felt so good to be in those familiar woods again. It was like coming home. But despite my excitement, a part of me was removed, distant, as though searching. A mild discomfort belied the joy I seemed to be experiencing. Everywhere we went, I found myself constantly scanning the old familiar places for something else. But what? Something was missing. But I could not put my finger on it. Something very important. But I just could not remember. Or perhaps it was the child still alive in me that did not want to remember. The child who had held the dearest creature in all his life hard against his cheek before kicking it hard in the ribs and running in tears to the waiting car. It was not until I came to a very special tree near the river—a tree I knew far better than the others—that my subconscious opened to reveal the most beloved and painful of all my memories on the farm. Bo. What I would have given to see him there, to hold him, to feel his hot wet tongue against my cheek just one more time!

Hurriedly, I took Wendy by the hand and we walked back to the car. I felt a little relieved as I returned to the present. Leaving the farm behind, we drove to the village only five miles up the road. The school I had attended was there. Or what was left of it.

The buildings that had housed the classrooms, the old water tower, and the cafeteria were all gone—apparently torn down years before. Only the slide and the old wooden merry-go-round—the one we used to chase the girls off of—were still there. The store at the end of the street where I would go to get sodas for my teacher was still standing, although a couple of men were methodically tearing it down, too. After taking pictures of what was left, I asked one of the men if he knew the Jones family. As luck would have it, he did. He told me Mrs. Jones was working in a clothing factory in a small town nearby. I could find her there.

Nervously, I entered the office of the factory a few minutes later. I did not know what to expect or what her response to my coming might be. There was a receptionist sitting at a desk.

"Would it be possible for me to speak to Mrs. Jones for a moment?" I asked tentatively.

"We are not supposed to disturb the employees unless it is an emergency," she said. "Can you wait until their lunch break?"

"It's not an emergency," I answered, "but it is very important that I talk with her now. I'll only take a minute. Please!"

After looking at me a moment longer, the woman leaned toward an intercom, pushed a lever, and announced for all to hear that Mrs. Jones had a visitor in the outer office.

A moment later she came through the door. My heart leaped into my throat as I recognized the woman who had played such an important role in my life so long ago. She was just as I remembered her, only older.

"Yes?" she asked. She looked from the woman at the desk to me.

For a long moment I could not speak. I just stood there staring at her, feeling emotions that were years old. I could tell she did not recognize me. But then, why would she? I was only a young boy then.

"Don't you know who I am?" I asked at last.

"No, can't say as how I do," she answered, looking hard at my face. "You wouldn't be the Parkers' oldest boy, would you?"

"No ma'am," I answered. "I'm Peter."

I thought she was going to faint. Her face turned white and she began to shake. I saw shock, surprise, curiosity, pain, wonder, and joy pass in turn through her eyes before some of the color returned to her face. She came up to me and wrapped her still-strong arms around me.

"Oh my G--!" she exclaimed under her breath. "I know'd you'd come back!" She was crying.

Wendy and I had dinner with the two of them that night on the farm. We ate in the living room and talked and talked. They wanted to know everything about what had happened to us boys and how my brothers were. It was only then I realized the Jones really had cared about us boys and tried to help. They never again took in foster children, they told me. The pain of losing us had just been too much. How strange it felt, sitting there as an adult, knowing for the first time that what you had wanted so desperately as a child was there all the time, but unrecognized!

At last I could stand the memories no longer and we prepared to leave, with the promise to stay in touch. Then I asked her if she knew where any of my biological family could be found. She did! She had stayed in touch with my father off and on over the years, hoping to hear some news of us.

I was stunned when the address she gave me was that of the house we had lived in before he and Mother divorced! From the bedroom window of that house, I had watched him leave with my older brother and sister that night when I was five years old. From that house, I had watched my mother being taken away in an ambulance the following day. The memories just kept coming, piling up and over one another until they became a blur.

We drove to the house that night. The shock of my sudden appearance out of nowhere on his front porch was no less for my father than it had been for Mrs. Jones.

For an hour we visited. But I could not relax until I had found the others. He, of course, knew where they all were. We called my older brother on the phone, since he was living in another state. It felt strange to talk with a brother I had not seen in fifteen years. We promised to try to get together soon.

Then my father took us to my mother. On the way, he told me she was not in the best of health and had been in and out of hospitals for years. I wanted to ask a thousand questions, but did not. He told me she was remarried, to the man she had brought with her when she came to visit us on the farm. And she had raised two more boys.

How desperately I wanted to love that woman, now old and grey, sitting across the room from me. The only thing I recognized were her smile and her hands. And the picture of Jesus hanging on the wall. When I asked if it was the same one she had when we were with her, she acknowledged that it was. I was so happy to see her! I could not control the emotion that came pouring out of me. But the part of me that I most wanted—no, needed—to respond to her lay cold and dormant inside. It was as though a part of me were dead. How hard it was to sit in the same room with my mother, desperately wanting so much and feeling so little.

It was not until much later that I came to realize my love for her was not dead at all, but buried deep in a child's memory where it would be safe and protected, preserved through all time. Having lost his mother three times as a child, the adult dared not risk claiming more than he already had, for fear of losing her again—and along with her, those precious treasured memories of the only real mother he ever had.

After saying farewell without so much as a hug, but promising to return at some future date, we were escorted by my father to my sister's house. She was not home from work when we arrived, so we sat in the driveway and talked. A few minutes later a pickup truck pulled into the driveway.

"Hello, Daddy," I heard her say as she stepped out of the truck. "What brings you over so late at night?"

"Let's go in the house," he answered. "There's someone here I want you to meet."

I watched her closely as she passed within inches of me in the darkness. She did not look at me, but I recognized her instantly—not by her face or hair. It was her teeth! My next younger brother had those same buck teeth! The last time I had seen her, I was still a child on the farm, and they had all come down to visit us that Christmas. How I had clung to her then, begging her not to leave me!

Once introduced, we fell into each other's arms and just stood there for a long time. No effort was made to break us apart. Maybe they all sensed the desperate love and yearning and need we had for each other that had never died. I don't know. But at last I was free to love my sister without fear and grief.

At last we sat down near each other on the couch and talked while pictures were taken. I could not get enough of her! Aching, searing love poured from me into her and back again. Once the dammed-up feelings were released, they gushed in a torrential flow that overpowered us both.

It was so hard to leave her that night. But at last I had to get away. The emotional impact of being reunited with all the members of my long-lost family was almost more than I could bear. I honestly wondered if I would survive the experience.

For hours afterward, I could not talk. Fortunately, Wendy seemed to understand and left me to my thoughts. I drove endlessly into the night with the window down and the cool air whipping against my burning face.

For two weeks after the reunion I stayed in bed, suffocating in a deep depression. Every sense was numb, all my feelings depressed to the point that I could not even care for myself. Day after day I just lay there, aching and hurting and trying to find, deep in my own thoughts, some way to survive.

At last life and feeling returned—slowly at first and then more intensely. And strange things began to happen. I became short-tempered and incredibly difficult. The smallest thing would send me into a rage. It was as if all my feelings were extremely sensitive to even the slightest stimulation. I began turning against Wendy and cursing her in my rage. I was terrified by what was happening to me. But the harder I tried to overcome it, the worse it became and the less control I seemed to have.

This continued throughout the summer as we made our final preparations for departure. And sadly, it continued once we were settled in the new town and I had begun my seminary work. But then occurred the most horrifying thing of all. I began doing to my two children what had been done to me as a child! I began hurting them in the ways I had been hurt. In horror and agony, I watched myself slowly but surely destroying their young, innocent lives. What little self-respect I had mustered through my academic achievements and my work with the kids in the ghetto school was gone. Bitterly, I hated what I was doing, and I quickly grew to loathe myself beyond any point I had ever experienced.

After a while it became clear to me that if I continued to hurt my children, sooner or later I would kill them. My rages were becoming increasingly more frequent. I decided then I could be a good father only by finding a way to protect my children from myself. I could see only two ways to do this. The first was to get as far away from them as possible. This I ruled out, because I could not bear the thought of not being with them. That left but one option. I would have to kill myself. That is what I decided to do.

As I was making plans and readying myself, I happened across a book on child abuse at the library. I read it. Then I seized and devoured every book on child abuse I could find.

Those few books were my deliverance! As I read, I could identify with what the authors were saying. They were talking about me! Through them, I began to understand more and more about what was happening to me. Even more important, through them I found the answer to my dilemma.

I did not need to kill myself. Nor did I need to kill my kids. All I had to do was give my children the same respect I would give another human being, or even another person's child. I would never dream of doing to your child what I was doing to my own. I would not do to my car what I was doing to my children. It would chip the paint! But somehow I believed I had not only a "right" to hit my kids, but a God-given responsibility to do so—as a means of controlling their behavior and making them into what I wanted them to be. All the acts of violence directed at them were justified and rationalized as the necessary parental response to some infraction on their part.

I learned from those books that I did not have a "right" to hit my children, or any child. Nor did I have a right to raise them any way I chose. They did not belong to me in the sense of a possession. They were ultimately God's children, given only into my temporary care. My responsibility as a parent was to build them up, not tear them down.

What I had to do was outlaw violence in all its forms in my family. Violence could not be tolerated for any reason. I would need to find nonviolent ways to discipline them. Just as important, I would need to find constructive ways to deal with my rage. With this understanding came a desire to learn more about my problem. That is when I began my study of child abuse.

The violence in my children's lives stopped completely about the time my daughter turned three years old. Most of it, or all of it, I hope, is buried in that time of childhood before recollection. Not once since then have I struck my children for any reason. I pray to God that neither of them can *ever* remember being hit by me!

Although there was much I had yet to learn about child abuse—why and how it happens—by outlawing violence in my family I had taken the first and most essential step in protecting my children and giving them the chance to have normal, healthy childhoods. By that single powerful act, I broke the cycle of abuse.

Twenty

It is not easy to admit that I, too, had become an abusive parent. Those memories are terribly painful. Yet failure to do so not only would have been deceitful, but would have ignored one of the most serious aspects of the abusive cycle.

Tragically, the legacy of child abuse is commonly passed from one generation to the next. Child-abuse victims tend to become abusers. Thankfully, there are exceptions. But not as many as you might think.

This really is not so hard to understand, if you consider for a moment how we learn to parent. Certainly we do not learn it in our schools, nor do we learn it at church or in other structured settings. Ultimately, we learn how to be parents by watching our parents. Unless we make a conscious effort to learn new techniques and skills, we tend to expect from our children what was expected of us; punish for the same reasons; and use the same kind of discipline with our children that was used with us. Combine this with the fact that our tolerance of violence increases with continuous exposure, and you have a situation in which survivors of childhood violence will tend to use violence in their own parenting. I was no exception. But unlike many others, I was able to break the cycle before it resulted in tragedy for my family.

I wish that I could honestly tell you that all the problems originating in my childhood were resolved when I entered seminary and outlawed the use of violence in my family. But I cannot. The lives of my children were preserved, and my relationship with them, but I still had to deal with myself.

Always before, I could hide, pretend to be someone else. During the past twenty-five years, I had grown to believe I was worthless and unlovable. Why else would people who were supposed to love me treat me the way they did? And why else would I do to my children what I did? Never before had anyone seriously challenged my personal identity. Until I entered the seminary community.

There, in the midst of those loving, caring, Christian people, I was forced to take a new look at just who and what I really was. I had always avoided taking a serious look at myself, for fear of what I would surely find. But how do you stand in the presence of God without becoming "self" conscious? How do you stand in the presence of love for any length of time without feeling loved? How many times do people have to reach out to you in genuine caring, and continue to reach out despite your defensiveness and rejection, before you begin to feel worthwhile? For me it took a lot!

Once when we were discussing the risk of reaching out in love, Father Paul had said, "If you are going to reach out your hand to another person, my son, expect from time to time to have a nail driven through it." How many nails did I drive through how many hands those first couple of years? And yet they kept coming! How fortunate I was to be blessed with some time in the midst of such people.

By my senior year, I began tentatively experimenting with loving and caring. Slowly and cautiously, I began reaching out. What I found startled me. The vulnerability of caring brought such a profound joy that the occasional pain it also brought was nothing in comparison!

For years I had dismissed other people's caring as naiveté. Wait until they get to know the *real* me and then we will see how much they care! I would tell myself. I did not know then that I was hating an illusion, whereas they were loving the real me. But by borrowing their eyes to take a closer look at myself, I began to perceive the difference. It was I, not they, who had been deceived for twenty-five years.

The seminary experience brought into full, agonizing view all the negative feelings and problems that had been simmering below the surface. They could no longer be denied or repressed. I had to deal with them. It was a difficult and turbulent three years. But never before or since have I grown so much in so short a time.

Totally absorbed in my studies, work, and personal metamorphosis, I completely neglected my marriage. During those years Wendy saw only the outpouring of those unpredictable, negative emotions that had held me prisoner in my own childhood. She did not see the beginning metamorphosis, the gradual identity changes, the occasional positive feelings taking shape. By the end of my senior year, our marriage was in ruins.

At the encouragement of Father Paul, after graduation from seminary I resigned my candidacy for Holy Orders and chose instead to continue my education. Although I had come far, I had an even greater distance still to go. But through seminary, I found the way. I was fortunate enough to be accepted into a doctoral program offered by the Divinity School at Vanderbilt University in Nashville, Tennessee. The week after graduation, we were on our way to Nashville.

For two years I worked as Christian education director in a large parish while pursuing my studies at Vanderbilt. It was during this time that Wendy gave up and decided she wanted out. She filed for divorce. I did not resist.

I do not blame her for leaving. I was not a good husband. She deserved so much more of what I did not give and so much less of what I did. She hung in there with me for ten years and we had two wonderful children. What more could I ask? I remember now the early days of our life together and something I would tell her again and again. I think it pretty well characterized me and my relationship with Wendy at the time.

"The root of all disappointment is expectation," I would tell her. "If you do not want to be disappointed in me, then do not expect anything of me!"

Isn't that sad? But at the time I really believed what I was saying. I could not stand the thought of disappointing her, as I thought I had disappointed every other person who had ever loved or cared about me—so much that they finally did not want me any more. I guess this was my way of making sure the same thing did not happen again.

After obtaining a doctorate from Vanderbilt, I began work in a local hospital as director of the Department of Pastoral Care. I was hospital chaplain and also maintained an active counseling practice. Although I had done my doctoral project in the area of child abuse, my specialty was counseling. Most of my counseling was in the area of marriage and divorce, but I was shocked by the number of people, particularly women, who told me at some point in the therapeutic relationship of having been physically, emotionally, or sexually abused. I got some idea of just how many of us there really are!

Then one day a civic leader called me.

"We are hearing a lot about this child abuse business lately," he said. "Will you have lunch with us at our club and talk to us about it?"

The man had no idea I was a victim. At first I wanted to decline his invitation. Mostly out of fear. Fear of what they would think of their chaplain if they knew the truth about his past, and fear of standing in front of a group to talk. But then I remembered the dream that had prompted me to quit my job with the estate-planning company and enter seminary. It was then I knew my purpose. I accepted the invitation.

After that first presentation, word spread. Before long, other invitations began to come in. And then more. I accepted them all. Soon I was traveling out of the county to speak, then out of the state. By June 1983, the demands on my time had become so great I was forced to choose between my work in the hospital and my work to prevent child abuse. I could not do both.

At that time, I left the hospital and founded ICARE (International Child Advocacy and Resource Enterprises). It was then, also, that I wrote *Cry Out!* Since then I have made more than three hundred talks and presentations in the area of child abuse all over the country.

I know my destiny now. After years of searching, I have found my place in the Kingdom. I know where I belong. I have committed my life to two purposes. The first is to be the very best father possible to my children, and friend to yours, should I encounter them. Second, I have committed my life and resources to stopping and preventing the needless tragedy of child abuse.

My work is somewhat unique in that I combine both clinical and experiential insights in the presentations. If we ever hope to accomplish our goal, it is not enough to simply capture the mind of the public. We must capture your heart as well. Only then will you know enough and care enough to do what must be done to stop the abuse of our children.

In addition, I do all my work from the victim's perspective—as a child advocate. This does not mean I am not also a parent and family advocate. You see, ultimately, because children need their parents and families, a child advocate *is* a family advocate. I stand against parents only occasionally, when parental rights conflict with the rights of the child. It is at those times that I stand firmly and steadfastly beside the child. Children are not capable of advocating for themselves, as are parents and organizations. For that reason, I lend them my voice.

When I speak of "child rights," I am not talking about political rights. I am talking about the right to have food to eat, clothes to wear, and a safe place to live. I mean the right to have their basic human needs met, to be loved, wanted, accepted, respected. The right to a happy and carefree childhood. The right to grow up in an environment free from danger, violence, exploitation, and abuse. The right to the privacy and sanctity of their minds and bodies, that neither will be raped, assaulted, or violated. This is what I mean by the rights of children. It is the birthright of every child. And it is the responsibility of every adult to see that these rights are respected.

There is a sense in which all the world's children are our own, just as their destiny will inevitably intertwine with ours. It is those young girls at this very moment being emotionally and sexually abused who will become the wives of our sons and mothers of our grandchildren. And the boys being abused will become the husbands of our daughters and fathers of our grandchildren. If we cannot protect them for their own sake, let us do so for the sake of our grandchildren! Those we fail to protect may fill our jails and prisons tomorrow. Or they may become our prostitutes, our drug addicts, our mental patients, our leaders in crime—rapists, murderers, thiefs, muggers—or at the very least, our suicides, as they live out their desperate lives of self-destruction.

It was not easy when I began, nor is it any easier now, to write or to stand before a group of people and talk about child abuse and my own experiences. It hurts. Even today it hurts. It will always hurt. But the pain of a survivor is small compared to the suffering of a victim. As long as there is an ear that will listen, or a heart that will care, or a mind that wants to know, I will continue. I, like so many others, have walked through hell to get this far. And I find I *do* have a voice and I *can* make a difference. There can be no looking away or turning back. I shall continue to lend my voice to the chorus crying out for mercy and compassion for all children, everywhere. And for the thousands who have died, I shall never cease to resist the madness that cost them their lives.

It is my sincere hope that this book and the one before it have so touched the hearts and minds of every one of you that you will join me and others in our effort to stop and prevent child abuse. If you are a parent who is abusing your child, stop before it is too late! Do it now, this moment. Vow to never again lay an abusive word or hand on your child. Do as I did—outlaw violence in your family. The peace and joy that comes from nonviolent family life will richly reward your effort and commitment. Know that the heart of a child, filled with self-hatred, bitterness, and loathing because of verbal and emotional abuse, will become the poisoned mind of an adult. Know that the distortion of a child's identity through sexual abuse will result in a disturbed personality in the adult. And know that the torturing of a child's body will result in a scarred and crippled adult shell, which seeks only to survive.

If you were a victim, know there is hope. You need not remain chained to the horrors of your childhood. It is possible to be set free of your past. Do not let your past rob you of your future. It is all you have left. Be sure the legacy you leave your children is one of love and peace, not pain and torment. Believe you can do it! And know there is a Power far greater than your own that makes all things possible. Life is to be lived, not survived. Claim your life as your own and live it! Let me know if I can help.

The American home is the most dangerous place in the nation. As children, we are taught to beware the stranger offering gifts and candy, and to avoid dark, deserted areas. Our parents dutifully prepare us at an early age for the unexpected that can occur outside the home. We are warned against the dangers that lurk on the street, around corners, and in dark alleys. Many times we are told there are people who would do us harm.

Tragically, the unexpected that occurs most often in the life of a child does not happen on the street, on deserted playgrounds after dark, or in a stranger's car. Nor is it performed by people with whom the child is not acquainted. The unexpected occurs most often in the child's own home and is done by parents and other familiar family members!

Family violence is one of the most serious social problems facing our country today, and it is present in one form or another in half of all families. Much of this violence is directed at those least capable of defending themselves—our children. Consider these sobering facts:

- family member killing family member is the most common type of homicide in our country;
- nearly one-third of all women slain are killed by the husband or boyfriend;
- an estimated 2,000 to 5,000 children will die at the hands of their parents or guardians this year;
- one out of every three females, and an almost equal number of males, will be involved in a sexually abusive relationship within the family before he or she reaches the age of sixteen;
- most women treated in emergency rooms have been beaten by the husband or boyfriend;
- most injuries or death to law enforcement officers are a result of attempted intervention in domestic violence situations;

- it is in the home that children are physically, sexually, and emotionally maltreated;
- it is in the home that husbands and wives beat and batter each other;
- it is in the home that divorces occur;
- more rapes occur in the victim's own home than anywhere else; and,
- it is in the home that, in one year, children can witness 10,000 acts of assault, rape, torture, and murder on routine evening television.

These statistics are not only shocking but frightening. Few of us can escape a life-threatening confrontation with crime, violence, and abuse on the street at some time in our lives. Sadly, even fewer of us can avoid it in our homes. Of paramount concern for all of us is the effect so much violence will have on our children.

An old axiom of human psychology suggests that tolerance is proportionate to exposure. The greater the exposure, the greater the tolerance. If this is true, can you imagine the tolerance toward violence we are building in our children? They watch people being beaten, battered, and murdered by every means imaginable. It is everywhere—in the movies, on television. It permeates our literature, is glamorized in sports, and even reflected in our art and music. It is romanticized, justified as a necessary means to a righteous end. We kill to prevent killing, use violence to prevent violence. We scream at our kids, "Don't scream at me!" We yell emphatically, "Don't hit!" as we sharply slap their hands.

Perhaps most disturbing of all are the heroes we create for our children. Men to whom we pay millions of dollars climb into a padded ring, put on padded gloves, and then proceed to beat other human beings into senseless submission, while we watch and cheer and capture it all on tape for future eyes to witness. What greater madness exists in modern society than our fascination, our obsession, our worship of violence and all it represents?

Is it any wonder domestic violence is the number-one health risk for families? Families are miniature imitations of the society within which they exist. What occurs at a societal level will surely be mirrored in the family; thus overwhelming social sanctioning of violence is reflected in a similar sanctioning of violence in the family.

Mental-health and child-development professionals generally agree that the adult personality is largely the result of childhood experiences. Well-adjusted adults tend to evolve out of well-adjusted children. The same is true for maladjusted adults. Children raised in home environments characterized by violence, degradation, and abuse will likely grow into deeply troubled adults, perhaps violent and abusive themselves. Violence perpetuates violence. There is no greater yet unacknowledged truth. Consider these shocking statistics:

- an estimated 80 percent of all abused children will become abusive parents. Children learn to parent by watching their parents;
- there are 1,500 people on death row in this country's prisons. Each of these was somebody's little boy or girl. Over 90 percent of these people were severely abused children; and,
- an estimated 80 percent of all persons convicted of violent crimes such as rape and murder were severely abused children.

The physical and mental torture of children in their own families can result in serious and perhaps irreversible consequences for all of society, including the child. Many seriously abused children who survive into adulthood adopt sociopathic life-styles which traumatize innocent victims all around them. Society pays, and pays dearly when children are abused—not only in terms of dollars needed to cope with the consequences, but the cost in terms of human misery and suffering is incredible.

Children's first experience of violence generally comes at the hands of their own parents in the form of what is euphemistically called a "spanking." These well-intentioned attempts at controlling the behavior of children can evolve into serious and life-threatening beatings inflicted upon the child. Just as alcoholism begins with the first drink, severe child abuse begins with the first blow. Telling potentially abusive parents that it is acceptable to "spank" their children is like telling an alcoholic it is all right to drink socially.

Over 90 percent of the American public believes it is acceptable for parents to use force and violence in their relationship with their children. There is even a belief among some parents that part of being a loving parent is the willingness to spank. Hitting children in the name of love teaches a definition of parental love that includes violence. Love never includes the willful infliction of pain and suffering.

Sadly, the issue in our current discussion of child abuse in this country is not *whether* we can inflict pain and suffering on our children. Instead, the issue is *how much* pain and suffering can we inflict before it becomes illegal, immoral, or unethical? How much hitting is too much? How much pain is too much? Where does a spanking end and a beating begin? When there is a bruise? A broken bone? A concussion? Blood? Somewhere along the continuum of not hitting a child at all and beating the child to death, we must draw a line and clearly separate parental prerogative from child abuse. Where do we draw the line?

Part of the tragedy of the "spanking that went too far" and the parent who "lost control" while administering corporal punishment—the most common cause of physical abuse in children—is that we do not need to use violence with our children. Corporal punishment is the least effective disciplinary tool. We truly can be good parents, effective parents, and raise well-disciplined children without laying a hand on them even once! But most parents do not know this.

They were spanked as children, told they deserved it, that it was done out of love. They grew up believing what they were told and model their own parenting after it. And so the cycle of violence is perpetuated into yet another generation. I was one of them. My parenting was modeled on my experience as a child. I was doing to my children what had been done to me.

Hitting is not the answer. There are other ways to raise children. Ways that relieve pain rather than inflict it. Methods that build up rather than tear down. I am talking about nonviolent parenting. Nonviolent parenting involves hugging, not hitting. It acknowledges and respects the basic human right of children to grow up in a world safe from violence and abuse; the right not to have their bodies, minds, or spirits violated by those more powerful. Nonviolent parenting is based on discipline rather than punishment. Its goal is to teach the child, not to control with fear and intimidation.

There is no room here, nor is it the purpose of this book to teach the methods of nonviolent parenting. But this is something that must be done. I believe most parents would choose nonviolent parenting if given a choice, if taught its skills and techniques, and if it has effective results.

Almost all parents want what is best for their children. They want childhood to be a precious, sacred time, free from life's endless problems and tragedies—a period of growth and development that will make possible an adult life filled with purpose and promise. Their concern is how best to provide such a childhood when there is so much to be taught and so little time to teach it. It is possible. It can be done through nonviolent parenting.

Child abuse starts in the family. It must stop in the family. Hitting is the root, the forerunner of all other forms of child abuse. As long as it is acceptable to violate a child's body, the right to violate the child's mind, spirit, and sexuality is only a rationalization away. If hitting is the problem, then not hitting is the solution.

221

There is a sense in which we all share in the abuse of children. We not only condone the use of violence as an acceptable, if not the preferred method of discipline, but we do nothing to stop it. We do not, however, share the pain of our children. The pain we feel is our own. It is the pain that comes from regret. It is the pain that comes from knowing there was another way, if only we had taken the time and made the effort to pursue it—a nonviolent alternative to the violence we chose. It is the pain that comes when violence by choice inflicted upon our children inevitably becomes violence by chance as we unexpectedly encounter its survivor—perhaps our spouse. Even more, it is the pain that comes when our children grow up to become just like us.

Once again I invite you—all of you—to join in the fight against child abuse. We cannot change the past, but we certainly can have something to say about our children's tomorrow. God knows they deserve the very best we have to offer. For what we have to offer is all they have.

For more information, write to:

ICARE
P.O. Box 499
Hermitage
TN 37076

Fontana, Vincent J. *Somewhere A Child Is Crying: Maltreatment—Causes and Prevention* (New York: Macmillan Publishing Co., 1973).

Gelles, Richard J. *Family Violence* (Beverly Hills: Sage Publications, 1976).

Justice, Blair, and Justice, Rita. *The Abusing Family* (New York: Human Sciences Press, 1976).

———. *The Broken Taboo: Sex in the Family* (New York: Human Sciences Press, 1979).

Kempe, Ruth S., and Kempe, C. Henry. *The Developing Child: Child Abuse* (Cambridge, Mass.: Harvard University Press, 1978).

Martin, Harold P., ed. *The Abused Child: A Multidisciplinary Approach to Developmental Issues and Treatment* (Cambridge, Mass.: Ballinger Publishing Co., 1976).

Piers, Maria W. *Infanticide: Past and Present* (New York: W. W. Norton & Co., 1978).

Quinn, P. E. *Cry Out!: Inside the Terrifying World of an Abused Child* (Nashville: Abingdon Press, 1984).

Stacey, William A., and Shupe, Anson. *The Family Secret: Domestic Violence in America* (Boston: Beacon Press, 1983).

Walters, David R. *Physical and Sexual Abuse of Children: Causes and Treatment* (Bloomington, Ind.: University Press, 1975).